AGELESS

Unless otherwise identified, all Scripture quotations in this publication are taken from the

Verses marked (NLT) are taken from the *Holy Bible, New International Version®* (NIV®). Copyright © 1973, 1978, 1984, 2011 by Biblica, Inc.® Used by permission of Zondervan. All rights reserved.

Verses marked (TPT) are taken from the The Passion Translation®. Copyright © 2017 by BroadStreet Publishing® Group, LLC. Used by permission. All rights reserved. thePassionTranslation.com.

Verses marked (MSG) are taken from The Message Bible. Copyright © 1993, 1994, 1995, 1996, 2000, 2001, 2002 by Eugene H. Peterson.

Verses marked (ESV) are taken from The Holy Bible, English Standard Version. ESV® Text Edition: 2016. Copyright © 2001 by Crossway Bibles, a publishing ministry of Good News Publishers.

Verses marked (MSG) are taken from The Message Bible. Copyright © 1993, 1994, 1995, 1996, 2000, 2001, 2002 by Eugene H. Peterson.

Verses marked (NASB) are taken from the *New American Standard Bible*. Copyright © 1960, 1962, 1963, 1968, 1971, 1972, 1973, 1975, 1977, 1995 by The Lockman Foundation.

Verses marked (Amp) are taken from the Amplified Bible Copyright © 2015 by The Lockman Foundation, La Habra, CA 90631. All rights reserved.

AGELESS

THE SECRET TO THE SPIRITUAL
FOUNTAIN OF YOUTH

MARIA DURSO

DEDICATION

I would like to dedicate this book to all the people
who have labored for years and feel like their
season of ministry is *over*—or slowly coming to an end.
I want you to know it's never over! Although you are growing
older chronologically and might feel like
you have "aged out," your spirit is *Ageless*. There is wisdom
that you have not yet tapped into and knowledge so deep that
must be passed onto the next generation of believers. The
presence of God and His word never ages.
We are carriers of His presence and His word.
So get ready because God is about to squeeze out
more of the anointing that has accumulated throughout
the years, and put you in places that you have never
ever imagined. This is what the church
needs for such a time as this.

You are *Ageless!*

TABLE OF CONTENTS

Dear Reader,

Allow me to introduce myself to you. My name is Maria Durso and I was born in 1950. I know what many of you are thinking, "Wow she's old and on her way out." I used to think exactly the same way. When I was in my twenties, and met the woman who is now my mother-in-law, I remember thinking, "Man she is the oldest woman ever." She was in her forties. The truth is, over the years, my precious mother-in-law taught me the keys to life more than anything I ever read in Vogue or Glamour magazine. While I needed everything she taught, she needed me just as much. I kept her young and current and she kept me sober minded and grounded. Four decades later, I am now the older woman with daughters-in-law of my own. Believe me when I tell you that life passes by in what seems like micro-seconds and before you know it the year of your birth will seem as ancient as 1950.

This brings me to why I'm writing this book. As I travel around the globe I meet women who were once active in their local church and they all seem to be singing the same song. It's more like a cry from deep within their heart, "Where is my place now that I'm older?" Many feel as though they have been replaced by the younger generation and now they're just standing on the sidelines watching life pass them by, not realizing that maybe they are just transitioning into a new season. I would even venture to say a far more valuable season in their lives. With a change of perspective, this new season could be a time to connect with those younger in the Lord, a time to mentor and mother, a time to be a spiritual parent and a time to pour out all that's been poured into them.

The Apostle Paul said in Galatians 4:19, "You are my dear children, but I agonize in spiritual labor pains once again until the Anointed One, will be fully formed in your hearts" (TPT). In 1 Thessalonians 2:8 Paul compares himself to a breastfeeding mother who shared not only the Gospel but also his very life. In the writings of the amazing Apostle Paul he gives us the secret to being Ageless, which is to give our very life to others. In black and white we discover God's true purpose for our lives and in turn discover the secret to the Spiritual Fountain of Youth. Our God is the Ancient of Days, yet He is as relevant today as He was from the beginning of time.

Our bodies might age, but our spirits are Ageless. I promise that when you drink from these sound biblical principles you will never feel dry, stale, outdated or old. You will also realize that what you thought was your end is just a new beginning. Let's embrace the season we are in, so out of us will flow the Ageless truths of God's word that are never outdated.

Love,

Maria

INTRODUCTION

I'D LIKE TO address the elephant in the room. There's a major separation, call it a great divide if you will, between the younger and older generations. Sadly, I've seen it creep into the church, causing a chasm, a huge void, in the holy flow of what God originally intended to build up the Body of Christ. The unification of the young and old brings a marriage of the best of both worlds. The older has the wisdom from years of experience and the younger has creativity in how to handle the wisdom so they can use it to change the world.

> Would you not agree that with age comes wisdom?

Would you not agree that with age comes wisdom? There are experiences that can only be shared by someone who has lived through them. It's those stories shared that gives us a peek inside of life's rhythm and what a disservice it is to not have those stories told. If you want to stop blood flow just put a tourniquet on your limbs. Stopping past life experiences from being shared would be no different. It would choke out all that has been stored up throughout the years, which were meant to enrich the present. Those stories were meant to be a breath of fresh air especially to the listener who is hearing them for the very first time. Unfortunately many older folks often think their experiences are not relevant or necessary to help the younger generation. These untold stories cause a generational gap.

Just imagine if delicious family recipes were never handed down from the previous generation. What in the world would we do at holiday time? On the flip side, those recipes that are handed down can be given a modern take on a classic when placed in the hands of a younger chef. The one that has held the classic recipe needs to release it as a blessing and shouldn't be critical when they see the preparation process being altered. We must wait until it is tasted and tested and maybe just maybe the change that was made just might be wonderfully refreshing.[1] That's how it is in the Body of Christ. We share our classic experiences and allow the younger believer to take it the way only they can and influence the culture at hand. Their influence draws people in with a fresh and fragrant aroma of Christ so that the outsider can come and feast at the table of the Lord, able to taste and see that the Lord is good.

On the other hand there are certain recipes that should never be touched. It would be like painting over the Mona Lisa. You cannot mess with perfection. We have such a recipe that has been in our family for four generations. It is called Pasta en Salada. It's a summer dish from Sicily. My husband's maternal grandmother handed it down to his mom and she handed it down to me. I have now handed it down to my daughter-in-law Yahris. Grandma's recipe comes out perfect every time. Similarly there are biblical principles that should never be tweaked or touched because the truth and principles in God's Word are always perfect. He has measured out the exact ingredients that enable us to live an abundant life.

The delicate part of this is in knowing what to enhance and what to leave alone. That's why we desperately need one another. Christianity is about relationship but the relationship is not only meant to be vertical, it is also meant to be horizontal.

As we grow in God, we should also grow in our relationships with one another and learn from one another in the process. Every Mary needs an Elizabeth. Every Ruth needs a Naomi. Every Timothy needs a Paul. But, let me just say, Elizabeth needed Mary, Naomi definitely needed Ruth, and the Bible clearly records how much Paul needed Timothy. Both brought out the best in each other. Simply put, we need one another more than we realize and we must allow each other to speak into our respective lives. We need what the generation after us has brought to the table and in turn, they need what we have to impart to them. As the generation that has gone before them, we must be transparent, vulnerable and not so self-righteous. However, the younger should be teachable and humble. We need to share our humanity with each other and all that it entails. We should share our weaknesses, trials and triumphs, and maybe just maybe we can help one another on this journey called life. As we impart our wisdom, we help the younger to mature, while they can help us to stay young, drinking from the spiritual fountain of youth. This unity broadens our horizons. We get to look into someone's eyes and see their soul. We get to refurbish the things that the elder might have discarded and discover the younger one's gift that has yet to be excavated.

Imagine if the younger generation said, "No thanks we have our own recipes, we really don't need what you have to offer." Or what if they said, "Give me the recipe but don't tell me how to make it." Or what if the elder said, "No I'm not parting with that recipe because I don't want anything to be changed," or "I will not hand it over because I don't believe you are able to handle it properly." That's how it feels when we shut one another out, what a travesty that would be.

Most importantly we the elder must learn the art of how to hand the recipe down. We can't force the younger generation to do it "our way" nor can we lord over them measuring every ingredient. We should want nothing more than to gently sway them to use the right elements. However they decide to change it up should be fine with us as long as the main ingredients are being used.

The Bible declares that older women should teach the younger, but the younger must be willing to be taught. We must all come to the conclusion that we don't know everything but what we do know we will gladly share with one another so that we can all step up our game.

"Two people are better than one, for they can help each other succeed. If one person falls, the other can reach out and help. But someone who falls alone is in real trouble" (Ecclesiastes 4:9-10).

Ageless = Teachable

CHAPTER ONE

AGELESS = FEARLESS

*"For God did not give us a spirit of timidity, but a spirit of
power, of love, and of self-discipline."*

2 Timothy 1:7

I WAS TERRIFIED to write my first book. At times, para-
lysis overtook me because the thought of any kind of
criticism, of what people would think of me or about what I
wrote felt overwhelming beyond belief. This irrational fear
was rooted in a memory from my past, a lie I believed about
myself. Many years ago I wrote something that I felt God
had given me, and I allowed someone I esteemed to read
it. The only comment she made after reading it was that I
used too many commas. She said nothing about the content.
This response, which felt like rejection, caused me to put my
pen down for decades. My reaction was fear, yet I had never
thought of myself as being a fearful person. As I look back
I would venture to say I sabotaged myself on many occasions
because I was so terrified to fail, but possibly even more
terrified to succeed.

Fear is a bully!

Fear is a bully! It's the gigantic, sometimes invisible, Goliath of our emotions, a thief that has robbed our years and has caused us to sabotage so many divine opportunities. The ultimate strangler of potential, it causes us to look at our inadequacies and compare ourselves to other people that we feel are more gifted, qualified, or according to our low self esteem, more highly favored by God.

Fear will cause us to stop dead in our tracks or even subtly back pedal through life. It will cause you to look at life through the rear view mirror crying over what we haven't done instead of looking at the plans God has for our life. Fear is no respecter of person, regardless of gender, age, or ethnic background it will do everything in its power to prevent you from being all that God intends you to be.

Now fear comes in many different forms. There is fear of the dark, fear of what the future has in store, financial fears, fear of illness, fear of failure, fear of criticism or fear of man as Proverbs 29:25 in The Message Translation says, *"The fear of human opinion disables; trusting in God protects you from that"* (MSG).

FEAR OF SURRENDER

Needless to say, these forms of fear are crippling. But there is one fear that is far more deadly and insidious than all those fears put together. It's the fear of surrender, of free falling into God's arms, trusting His plan for your life without any reservation. Surrender means, "to give up something completely or agree to forgo especially in favor to another person."[2] As Christians, I believe our greatest fear is not to

The enemy
of our soul
wants us to
live fearful,
but God
wants us to
live fearless!

die but to live a totally surrendered and abandoned life to God, for God. Fear to let go of our life, as we know it. Fear to die to self and live for others. Fear to believe God and take Him at His word.

The enemy of our soul wants us to live fearful, but God wants us to live fearless! In fact, God provides the way by giving us His very own Holy Spirit to propel us forward as we walk in His power, might and strength. We somehow have reduced living for God to "attending church on Sunday" as an extra added bonus to our daily routine. But that's just a start, *real living starts with dying*—dying to self! John 12:24 (NIV) states, *"Very truly I tell you, unless a kernel of wheat falls to the ground and dies, it remains only a single seed."* Seed never produces a harvest unless it first falls to the ground and dies. Matthew 10:39 states, *"If you cling to your life you will lose it. But if you give up your life for me, you will find it."* In The Message Translation, it reads, *"If you don't go all the way with me, through thick and thin, you don't deserve me. If your first concern is to look after yourself you'll never find yourself. But if you forget about yourself and look to me, you'll find both yourself and me."* Do you truly believe that? That's the question to ponder because our glorious spiritual future hinges on dying to self today. I didn't say this was easy by any stretch of the imagination.

How do we forget about self when self is who we are? This seems next to impossible because these scriptures are telling me that in order to get an increase there has to be a decrease. The word "lose" is always associated with a deficit. No one ever wants to lose, except weight of course! Each and every one of us was born with the instinct of self- preservation (me first, you second). But Jesus says it plain and simple, if you want to be first then you have to be second. The way up is down. This makes absolutely no sense to the human mind, not to mention it's a little scary. Piggybacked on our fear of dying to self is our fear of connecting with others, especially those that are different than we are. We are afraid to be transparent and vulnerable; fearful of our minor differences instead of finding comfort in the things we have in common. Evidence that His thoughts and ways are *nothing* like ours.

FEARLESS LIVING

What does living fearless for God look like? Let's go to the source and find out starting with, what makes God tick? What are His likes? What gets God going? We are made in His image and likeness, so it stands to reason that whatever gets God going will get us going as well. What satisfies God will satisfy us.

From the beginning of time God has been in the people business. He cared about people more than He cared about His own life. This is something we can all apply to our own life. God, who owns heaven, which is prime real estate I might add, wasn't walking around heaven saying, *"Wow*, this is mine all mine. Look at those streets of gold, those pearly gates and oh those walls of jasper." No way! He wasn't satisfied owning heaven unless He had someone to share it with. Think about this, God Himself, who is the anointing, wasn't satisfied until He had someone to pour that anointing into. He wasn't satisfied until He saw Himself replicated in someone else's life. God needed to be in relationship with us. He desired to make contact with man so we could know His very heart and He was willing to pay the ultimate price in order to have this connection with us. He had to decrease so that increase could come.

God created Adam and Eve in His own image and likeness. He would walk with them in the cool of the day. He set them in a climate controlled luscious garden. And when they fell He didn't cut them off, no He covered them up and devised the ultimate plan to redeem all of mankind so that mankind would know how much He wants to be with them. The plan was costly, because He had to part with His one and only Son for a time. Jesus had to pay the ultimate price for a fallen humanity in order for mankind to be restored back to their creator. He was the ransom, the scapegoat because we all have failed but the Father didn't cut us off. He covered us up, and wrapped us in robes of Jesus' righteousness.

The Apostle Paul shared his heart with the fellow believers in 1 Thessalonians 2:8, *"We loved you so much that we shared with you not only God's Good News but our own lives, too."* Paul had life because he was pouring out his life. Do you think God saved Paul just to give people doctrine and theological facts? No, He saved Paul so that he could represent Jesus on this earth. Isn't that why we are saved? Did God put all that anointing inside of Paul just to give out doctrine? No, Paul was continually plugged into the invisible source, the Holy Spirit. He always had a current of life flowing through his veins. Out of that current came electricity to be connected to the people God loved. If Paul's life were seen on a TV screen you would see...

"My dear children, for whom I am again in the pains of childbirth until Christ is formed in you" (Galatians 4:19, NIV).

He was standing in proxy as a surrogate mother carrying their burdens. When you look through scripture you see that God calls himself Father—*Our Father who art in heaven*—He was about a family and God's family is the Body of Christ. His description is personal and relational. God is

> Fearless living means believing that you are that life and your life matters. Do you believe it?

more than someone in the sky spitting out rules and regulations. He is a caring God. He even compares Himself to a mother in Isaiah 49:15 (NIV), *"Can a mother forget the baby at her breast and have no compassion on the child she has borne? Though she may forget, I will not forget you!"* God is in it to win it—so looking at the source of life we must be connected to the Body—the Family of God. We are living at a time where the church is missing spiritual fathers and mothers.

Fearless living is loving others more than we love ourselves and taking God at His word, knowing that what God says He can do through one surrendered life, He will do! Fearless living means believing that you are that life and your life matters. Do you believe it?

WHY SO DRY?

When we are asked, "How are you doing?" our reply oftentimes has been, "Just hanging in there," because we feel like we are barely getting by. In the current Internet world that we live in, we have teaching via sermons or bible studies at our fingertips 24/7. We have "how to" books for every stage and every age of our Christian journey. Yet we go through greater periods of dryness than the generations before us. With all this Good News you have to wonder why we as Christians oftentimes find ourselves so dry? Have we become just a well of stored up information? Has God created us and sent His Son for us to "just hang in there?" Aren't we supposed to be "more than conquerors?" Is life today harder than it was for the previous generations? It certainly is not harder for us than it was for the apostles. They suffered persecution, physical beatings, were ostracized from their peers, and so much more (2 Corinthians 4:7-9). They did not have access to video or audio recordings of Christ's teachings to refer to. No book had been written at that time on how to love your obnoxious neighbor or how to be gracious to the neighborhood adulterer. We, on the other hand, have all of life's conveniences to assist in our spiritual growth and yet we find many believers going from one dry spell to another. Why is this?

The solution isn't as complex as it would seem. As a matter of fact it's rather obvious. In order to find the cure for dryness we must once again go to the source. The answer can be found by looking at the one who made us into His image and likeness. We have learned that God is in the people business. Proverbs 8:31 states, *"People are His delight"* (NIV, paraphrased). This tells me that we are never more like God than when we fearlessly love people, more than our possessions, comfort, and even our very own life. God has now placed us into the people business or should I say, His people's business. It also tells me that we will never be more satisfied than when we are living our lives for others.

Another reason for going through a "dry spell" is that you might be living on yesterday's blessings rather than believing God for a new move of His Spirit in your life. Perhaps you have lost your passion and have settled for merely existing in the memories of the past rather than grabbing hold of a new and vibrant experience with God. When we settle we accept a less desirable alternative. We should never settle for less! If you settle for less of God, then you will take in more of the world and before long you won't have anything worthwhile to share with others. The more of the world we allow into our lives the more opportunity for fear to dictate the course of our life and the thought of dying to self becomes unfathomable. I don't know about you but I've come too far with the Lord to allow myself to settle for less when God has promised life more abundantly. In turn, when we start living the abundant life, we want to share what God is doing with others.

If you have received Christ into your life then He lives on the inside of you by the power of the Holy Spirit. He promised to pour out His Spirit on *all flesh*. His power gives us the courage to live life beyond our own ability and personal needs. We can agree together not to allow the fear of dying-to-self bully us any longer. Instead let's live for others, by faith, on His behalf. I truly believe that if you take care of God's business, He will take care of yours. I guarantee that you will never be shortchanged when it comes to the economy of heaven. There is something about obeying the promptings of the Holy Spirit during the day instead of focusing on yourself that will take you on a glorious adventure of joy unspeakable! It's so addicting that it almost becomes selfish. Imagine that, selflessness becomes selfish because of what it does for you and your spiritual adrenaline. To that I say, "Let the joy begin!"

Today is
the day to
start living
fearlessly!

It's time that we take careful inventory of our own hearts so that we can detect the source of our dryness. Paul states in 2 Corinthians 13:5 (NIV), *"Examine yourselves to see whether you are in the faith; test yourselves. Do you not realize that Christ Jesus is in you—unless of course, you fail the test?"* Knowing that Christ is in us should make us *fearless.* That truth alone should give us the concern and courage we need to be a *giver.*

Fear will keep you invested in yourself instead of being invested in others. It will manipulate you with a "what if mentality," causing you to live in the negatives instead of the positives. Fear considers the impossibilities while faith sees what's possible with God. When you live in fear you will get drier and drier as the days go by. But when you live with eyes of faith you will begin to see new life, hope and joy spring up out of the well of your soul! Today is the day to *start living fearlessly!*

AGELESS QUESTIONS

1. List one time when fear bullied you and kept you from stepping out in faith.

_____

_____

_____

_____

_____

2. Has some criticism or discouragement stopped you dead in your tracks? Explain.

_____

_____

_____

_____

_____

_____

_____

_____

_____

_____

_____

_____

_____

_____

3. What does *fearless living* for God look like in your life?

_____

_____

_____

_____

_____

_____

_____

_____

_____

_____

_____

_____

4. The Bible states in Genesis 5:1 (NIV), *"When God created mankind, he made them in the likeness of God."* What does that mean to you?

_____

_____

_____

_____

_____

_____

_____

_____

_____

_____

_____

5. What do you do when you hit a "dry spell" in your faith journey?

_____

_____

_____

_____

_____

_____

_____

_____

_____

_____

6. Would you consider yourself to be giver – invested in the
   lives of others? Give an example of how you invest your
   time, talents and treasures in others.

_____

_____

_____

_____

_____

_____

_____

_____

_____

_____

_____

_____

_____

CHAPTER TWO

AGELESS = FRESHNESS

"New wine calls for new wineskins."

Mark 2:22b

I HAVE TWO neighbors nearby, both of whom are up in age. Their children have all grown up and moved away. One of them is cheerful, the other not so much. One of them keeps her home updated with small changes and upgrades as necessary. She is always inviting guests over to her home, and the smell of freshly baked cakes and pies permeate throughout the rooms. The other neighbor's home smells stagnant. She doesn't notice the staleness because she has lived in it for so long and never has company to point it out to her. She never thinks to make the necessary changes that are needed because change isn't something she considers. One neighbor is stuck in the past, while the other sees her future still in front of her.

The question I have for you is: do you want the home of your heart to be stale and stagnant or have the sweet aroma of life that is pleasing in the nostrils of God? The choice is yours, but a life of freshness will require an intentional change of mind and heart. Change will mean that you need to examine your input and output when it comes to relationships and the impact you have on those around you.

GOD MAKES ALL THINGS NEW

"Look, I am making everything new!" Revelation 21:5

Nothing will age you more than living stuck in the past. You could be hung up on something that happened in the past, or be attached to the way things used to be done. The Bible tells us that Jesus is the same *"Yesterday, today and forever,"* but that doesn't mean that we should remain the same. The Good News is all about transformation. Our relationship with God is not to remain the same and become stale, but should be ever evolving so that there is evidence of life, passion and purpose. It's been said the "proof is in the pudding" which means that you can only judge the *quality* of something after you have tried, used, or experienced it. In order to be ageless we need to be willing to let go of the "old" and experience the "new." Getting stuck in our own view of something rather than putting on the lens of the Spirit can trip us up, and even contribute to a limited understanding of scripture.

Have you ever read a scripture in God's sacred word only later to learn that you completely misunderstood what it meant? Even worse, when someone would preach from that specific text it would irritate you. There was one verse in particular that annoyed me and made me feel uncomfortable, uneasy, and if I'm honest, made me feel like yesterday's leftovers. In general, I'm not that kind of person. I love God's word and above all I love the Lord, so there have been very

Do you want
the home
of your heart
to be stale
and stagnant
or have the
sweet aroma
of life that
is pleasing
in the nostrils
of God?

few times where His Word would cause me to stiffen my neck and resist Him.

Whenever I have heard the verse: *"New wine calls for new wineskins"* in Mark 2:22b, I felt it pitted the old against the young. I used to love this scripture back when I was the new kid on the block, but now that I'm not so young I had come to resent it. It made me feel pushed out, useless and disposable. While my ear heard the words of the scripture, my heart heard, "out with the *old* and in with *new*." It was as though older saints had an expiration date, and the Holy Spirit couldn't fill believers that have been around the block a time or two. I began to ask if the "new wine" was reserved for the young? Was it only reserved for those who wear skinny jeans?

I knew God absolutely used older people. Look at Abraham and Sara for example. Abraham was seventy-five years old when God first revealed Himself to Abram. Then at the age of one hundred, his ninety-year-old wife, Sara gave birth to their son. Abraham lived to one hundred and twenty years old. Elizabeth, the mother of John the Baptist, was eighty-eight years old when she gave birth to him. Moses was eighty years old when he saw the burning bush, a monumental moment which catapulted him into his destiny. And then there's Enoch. He lived to be 365 years old and Methuselah lived for 939 years.

FRESH VS. STALE

After four decades of misunderstanding this scripture in Mark 2:22, I finally decided to do a study on it, and as the Holy Spirit would see fit, I saw this verse in a totally different light. To my surprise it has absolutely nothing to do with age. It has nothing to do with culture either. It's *not old vs. young,* but rather it's *fresh vs. stale.* In the English Standard Version it reads, *"new wine is for fresh wineskins"* (ESV). Let's put this in context. When Jesus said these words he was speaking to the religious people of the day who were stuck in a religious rut. These religious people couldn't accept any kind of change or shift in the way the winds of heaven were blowing. Do you know that it's the wind that is responsible for the change of seasons? People think it's the sun, but it's the wind, or what meteorologists refer to as the jet stream, that causes a change in temperature. We also know that a change in seasons means a change in clothes. The clothes that keep you warm and protected in January will suffocate you in June. Figuratively speaking, the religious people needed a change of clothes because it was a new season. The Messiah had come, the one they claimed to be waiting for, but they didn't recognize Him. They were suffocating in their orthodoxy and remained clueless. They not only didn't recognize Him, they fought against everything Jesus was doing. They were *stale*, *stiff*, and *stuck*. Much like I was when I came across the wine skin verse.

Then Jesus comes and shakes everything up, turning their programs upside down and makes a huge adjustment in what was known as ministry. He places people at the center and ministers to them according to their needs. This made them feel uncomfortable and revealed their lifeless Sabbath rituals. Jesus comes along and moves heaven's business onto the streets.

The word "new" as in "new wine" is the Greek word *neos*, which means "brand new."[3]

- Brand New Outpourings
- Brand New Infillings

- Brand New Empowerment

- Brand New Season of Anointing

- Brand New Holy Spirit Intoxications

The apostle Paul says in Ephesians 5:18, *"Do not get drunk on wine, which leads to debauchery. Instead, be filled (or be filled up or continually filled) with the Spirit"* (NIV, paraphrased). This is a command, not a suggestion. Yet it implies we have a choice. Just like someone who is intoxicated on alcohol, so we, when filled up with a brand new outpouring from heaven, will walk, talk and see things differently. When we are filled we will receive brand new revelations, brand new direction, and brand new unction. This *new wine* comes only from heaven and it's heaven's potion to replenish our strength. There's no substitute for the *new wine*. No man made elixir will do, it cannot be duplicated. No program can replace the *new wine*. We as believers need to be continually filled up because life depletes our strength. Just like a car runs out of gas and has to be filled back up, so we run low needing fresh, brand new infillings to give us vision and purpose.

The word "new" as in "new wineskins" is the word *kainos* in the Greek.[4] This word has a different meaning. This word means:

- Fresh

- Refreshed

- Renewed

- Revived

- Rejuvenate

This definition is stating that something that exists already can be made fresh or strong again. It is implying that only a refreshed, revived, rejuvenated wineskin can handle the new wine. Otherwise, like the Pharisees, we will miss the new (fresh) moves of God on the earth. God is always faithful to pour out new wine but it's our responsibility to maintain the condition of our inner man (wineskin) in order to receive that new wine.

> Regardless of your age you can be stale or fresh, it doesn't matter if you are young or old, what matters is the condition of your wineskin.

Regardless of your age you can be stale or fresh, it doesn't matter if you are young or old, what matters is the condition of your wineskin. The word fresh is the word of the hour. Everywhere we turn we see the word *fresh*. We see ads for *fresh* fruit...*fresh* vegetables...*fresh* juices...*fresh* food... makeup that leaves you looking *fresh*...and how about the ads that beckon us to *refresh* our wardrobes. *Why?* What's the "big deal" with having everything *fresh?* Because *stale* is not an option! Let's think about this for a moment. If in fact stale is not an option in anything we either put into or onto our bodies, doesn't it stand to reason that the part of us that is *most important* be kept *fresh?* Shouldn't our inner man (spirit/heart), the place where we commune with God and hear the voice of the Holy Spirit, be kept *fresh?* You may be asking yourself if it's possible for your spirit to become *stale?* I believe that it is not only possible it's probable. Our inner man needs daily care. It must be refreshed everyday. The same way we are deliberate to shower on the outside to clean the dirt or film of the day from our bodies, we must give our inner man a good cleansing, making it *fresh* once again on a daily basis.

It is worth repeating, age is not a factor, young and old alike must maintain the condition of our inner man. Jesus' mother, Mary, was young. She was a teen as a matter of fact. Jesus interrupted her life's program. Yet her wineskin was able to receive the new wine that heaven was pouring out. Her attitude was, *"let it be done unto me according to thy word."* At the end of her life she was in the Upper Room waiting for the promised Holy Spirit to fall. Look at the prophet Samuel, at a young age he heard the voice of God and said, *"speak Lord, your servant is listening."* Yet even in his old age it was said of Samuel, "not a word he spoke ever fell to the ground." No matter our age, young or old, we don't have to lose our thirst for a fresh outpouring.

FAITH, FIRE & FOCUS

I want us to look at two impressive characters in the Bible. The first one is Elisha. In 2 Kings 13 he had already been serving God for sixty-three years and he had never lost his *faith, fire or focus*. He was still as on fire at the end of his life as he was in the beginning. Remember in 1 Kings 19:19-21 when the prophet Elijah finds Elisha working in the field. Elijah takes off his cloak (mantle) and places it on Elisha symbolizing that Elisha was to replace Elijah for that generation. As soon as that mantle touches his shoulders he slaughters all his oxen, twelve yoke which were twenty-four oxen in total. He then proceeds to burn the wooden plow used for the family business to till the ground so that he could make a fire to roast the oxen for the whole town. Elisha was burning his livelihood. His family business was huge. The reason he was plowing with twelve yoke of oxen was because there was a huge amount of land. Yet because his wineskin was in a refreshed state he receives this fresh outpouring from heaven. He was burning all his bridges so that he would have nothing to go back to. Elisha is letting the town know that he was all in, with no back up or contingency plan. How many people get saved and have contingency plans? They keep the digits from past relationships just in case.

When my husband and I got radically saved we threw out all the drugs, drug paraphernalia, clothes, magazines, music, etc. But the one thing I held on to was watching Soul Train on Saturday morning. Remember Don Cornelius? I loved to dance and I would watch to learn the latest dance moves. I was at my first club by fourteen years old. I even found dance clubs open on Saturday afternoon. I don't know if it was a conscious decision or if subconsciously this was my contingency plan just in case this Christianity thing didn't work out. One Saturday as I was watching Soul Train, the Holy Spirit clearly spoke to me in a gentle voice, *"Maria what are you doing? You don't need to watch that because you are never going back there again."* That was the last time I ever watched that show.

In 2 Kings 13 we find Elisha sixty-three years later on his deathbed. He's still all in, having never lost his *faith, fire or focus.* The young King Jehoash comes to visit the prophet. He's weeping because he knows the prophet's days are numbered. He also knows the prophet's presence on earth has kept Israel safe in battle. While visiting the prophet the king sees a chariot and charioteers coming for Elisha. This must have been the same chariot that Elisha saw that came to take his predecessor, Elijah. But Elisha was not ready to go as he still had some anointing left in him. I'm sure he felt he needed to pass it on to someone else, just like it was passed onto him. This wasn't a time to weep it was time for war! Elisha was more alive on his deathbed than the young king was in his prime. The young king is *stale* but Elisha is *fresh*. Remember this is the king that quit striking the ground after 3 times. Elisha was furious. He doesn't know what it is to quit. His wineskin isn't shriveled up. He's the same prophet in 2 Kings 4 that went into the dead boy's room after Gehazi took his staff and prayed a *stale* prayer with no results. Then Elisha shut the door and wouldn't take no for an answer, he laid on top of the boy, eye to eye, mouth to mouth. He stretched himself out and the boy grew warm. Elisha got up, walked around the room and got back on the boy. He didn't quit at warm. The boy opened his eyes and sneezed seven times. Elisha had so much anointing in him that even after he died a dead man was thrown into his grave. When he fell on top of Elisha's bones he came back to life. Even though we go on to glory, the anointing inside of us never dies. It lives on. Our words and actions live on and still have quickening power.

And then there's Caleb, who at eighty-five years young, says, *"Give me the hill country."* No retirement for him. He says in Joshua 14:10b-12a, *"Today I am eighty-five years old. I am as strong now as I was when Moses sent me on that journey, and I can still travel and fight as well as I could then. So give me the hill country, the land the Lord has promised me."* Do you know that the hill country was the hard places? It was the place the enemy hid. It was steep and treacherous, yet that was the land that Caleb wanted. He could have said, "give me a nice plot of land so I can set up my tent and reminisce about the good old days. But that was not Caleb. The Bible says in Numbers 14:24, *"Caleb had a different spirit."* His spirit was continually drinking from the spiritual fountain of youth that never runs dry and will keep us *ageless*. We need to

We need to celebrate those who stood the test of time and have weathered a storm or two, those that haven't lost their *faith, fire* or *focus* even though the enemies of their faith have tried its hardest.

celebrate those who stood the test of time and have weathered a storm or two, those that haven't lost their *faith, fire* or *focus* even though the enemies of their faith have tried its hardest.

FRESH WINESKIN

So what exactly is a wineskin? A wineskin is a vessel that is fashioned or shaped to hold wine. Coincidentally it is shaped as the organ of the heart. Its purpose was to be a vessel that held wine and a person would carry the wine wherever they went. A healthy wineskin is expandable, pliable, supple and has give. It has the ability to yield to the new wine. It makes room for the new wine to expand because new wine always ferments.

Symbolically our wineskin is our inner man. Our spirit was created to carry around the *new wine* of the gospel. Wine symbolized joy. Joy for the journey. Our inner man was created to bubble up, carrying around the joy of the Lord wherever we go because the *"the joy of the Lord is our strength"* as it stated in Nehemiah 8:10b. No matter what's coming our way— *joy.* No matter how God chooses to move—*joy.* No joy = no strength. No strength, and we shrivel up.

Allow me to give you some wineskin facts:

- In order to keep a wineskin healthy it had to be carefully soaked in water so that all the sediment could be removed. The sediment was the dirt that was accumulated along the way. So with us, because the dirt of life accumulates along the way, we must be soaked in the water of God's Word. The psalmist writes in Psalm 119:25, *"I lie in the dust, revive me by your word."* God's word loosens the dust that settles in our heart.

🌿 The wineskin also had to be massaged with oil, carefully rubbing it into all the dry cracked places, restoring it back to it original state. Do you know that in Psalm 23:5 where it says, *"you honor me by anointing my head with oil,"* the original translation reads, *"you fertilized my head with oil, you nourished me for growth."* The oil of God's presence revives us as it soaks into our spirits.

🌿 The wineskin had to be maintained otherwise the new wine would leak out, therefore, the wineskin always had to be prepared for life's journey. When the wineskin is not replenished, it becomes stiff and hard.

When we are not soaking in God's presence and when we don't get a good soaking in God's Word, we become stiff and resistant to the move of the Holy Spirit. Fear replaces faith and works replace grace. We become shriveled up looking like sour prunes. Let's face it, if we're not soaking, we're sulking. Our spirit becomes incompatible with the New Wine and thus we become stuck and stale. Paul says in 2 Corinthians 4:16b, *"Though our outer man is decaying (or growing old), yet our inner man is being renewed (refreshed, rejuvenated), day by day"* (NASB, paraphrased). The inner man is getting a facelift. Paul is saying, I may be accumulating some wrinkles on the outside, but on the inside I'm a spring chicken. On the inside I'm standing tall like a runway model that's six feet tall. People should want a drink of what we're drinking! The world doesn't need some dried up old sour prunes. It certainly doesn't need some old stale religion. It needs a fresh outpouring. They need us to be intoxicated with the New Wine from heaven. We need to be vessels that carry around the New Wine of grace and joy, not the old stale wine of law and condemnation.

But those who wait upon God get fresh strength. They spread their wings and soar like eagles. They run and don't get tired they walk and don't lag behind (Isaiah 40:31, MSG).

I know that you feel just like me—we want our wineskins to be revived continually. In Joel 2:28-29 and Acts 2:17-19, both the old and new testaments declare, "I will pour out my Spirit upon all people. Your sons and daughters will prophesy. Your old men will dream dreams, and your young men will see visions."

It is up to us to be quality containers to carry the *new wine*! My prayer is that the Lord would give us new wineskins so we can receive the new wine … pour it out …pour it out…pour it out…*refresh us…revive us…rejuvenate us through and through*. Amen.

AGELESS QUESTIONS

1. How do you view yourself? Have you become *stale* in your approach and ability to share the Good News of the gospel or would you consider yourself as someone that takes the necessary precautions to remain *fresh*? Explain.

_____

_____

_____

_____

_____

_____

_____

_____

_____

_____

_____

_____

_____

2. Do you think age is a factor in getting stale or remaining fresh? Explain.

_____

_____

_____

_____

_____

_____

_____

_____

_____

_____

_____

_____

_____

_____

3. In Matthew 9:17 (ESV) reads, *"Neither is new wine put into old wineskins. If it is, the skins will burst and the wine spilled and the skins are destroyed. But new wine is put into fresh wineskins, and so both are preserved."* Why is it important that both the new wine and wineskins are preserved?

_____

_____

_____

_____

_____

_____

_____

_____

_____

_____

_____

_____

4. What are some practical ways to maintain the condition of your inner man?

_____

_____

_____

_____

_____

_____

_____

_____

_____

_____

_____

_____

_____

5. Is there a scripture that irritates you and if so could it be that you might not understand its meaning and intent? Write out that scripture and explain why it irritates you.

_____

_____

_____

_____

_____

_____

_____

_____

_____

_____

_____

_____

_____

CHAPTER THREE

AGELESS = TIRELESS

"Let us not grow weary of doing good, for in due season
we will reap, if we do not give up."

Galatians 5:9 (ESV)

THE WORD *WEARY*, as defined in Miriam-Webster's dictionary, means to be exhausted in strength, endurance, vigor or freshness.[5] As believers who work for the Lord, we can all attest to seasons of weariness. The author of the book of Hebrews is unknown but what we do know is that these Jewish believers living in Rome were under great pressure to return back to religious orthodoxy. On top of the fact that they were Jews and hated by the Romans, they were living a Christian life in a very secular society. I'm certain they were growing *weary*. It seems that the author is trying to prevent those he's addressing from abandoning their Christian faith by returning to Judaism. Before Christ, they were under the law and serving God was more of a duty, a religious checklist of sorts. Love was not the dominant motive. But once Christ came into their lives, motives changed and everything sprung out of His love. There was a fountain of grace springing up inside of them, instead of a fountain of law.

Think about your own life before you knew Christ. There are those of us who came out of denominational backgrounds and were nominal in our beliefs where we "served" God just like the Hebrews. There were religious holy days where we went to church, received ashes on our forehead and even fasted something we loved for a set amount of days all in an effort of gaining favor with God. We fit God into a nice neat box and made sure there was never any spillage into the rest of our lives. You could say our faith was contained with boundaries in place that God was not to cross.

On the contrary, serving God out of love becomes a whole different story. Love can't be contained to certain days or times. The Holy Spirit living inside of us isn't watching the clock or concerned with a certain image we might be trying to uphold. He continues to challenge us to do random acts of kindness for people we know and those we don't, anytime, anywhere. He presses us to give of ourselves and that could be a thankless job. It's the act of loving people when we are not loved back that can be very exhausting on us mentally, emotionally and spiritually.

KEY TO BEING AGELESS

The writer of Hebrews is a conduit of the Holy Spirit that wants to encourage them. His purpose is to send them winds of refreshing and to persuade them not to give up. He also points to, what I like to call, the *key to being ageless*, by inspiring them with these promising words:

"For God is not unjust. He will not forget how hard you have worked for him and how you have shown your love to him by caring for other believers, as you still do. Our great desire is that you will keep on loving others as long as life lasts, in order to make certain that what you hope for will come true. Then you will not become spiritually dull and indifferent. Instead, you will follow the example of those who are going to inherit God's promises because of their faith and endurance." Hebrews 6:10-12

As we look at this passage of scripture more closely, there are a few things I want to point out:

- *"God is not unjust"* – He is a just God!

- He will not forget how hard you have worked for Him— others may forget and may be oblivious, they may not see or be aware. They may even overlook you *but God* is taking notes, applauding your efforts and is pleased with you. Isn't it amazing how God forgets our short-comings and casts our sins into the sea of forgetfulness[6], yet he doesn't forget how hard we have worked for Him? Do you know that *God appreciates you*? So *don't get discouraged...Don't allow yourself to feel unappreci- ated...*because *your labor of love is not in vain.*

- Notice it says, *"How hard you worked."* You may be thinking, but I thought we were saved by grace and not by works? At least that's what it states in Ephesians 2:9. I thought it was nothing but the Blood of Jesus. Yes, that is all true. But on the flip side, our love for Him and our faith in Him causes us not only to work, but also to work hard *for Him*. Faith without works is dead (see *James*

2:14). Show me your faith, and I'll show you my works (see James 2:18).

🖝 We don't work hard to gain His approval, yet because we have His approval, we work hard! And He notices just how hard we do work and the great energy and effort we put into the work.

🖝 Beyond that it says, *"How hard you worked for Him."* For *Him...It's for Him...*Don't ever forget why you do what you do, it's for Him. It's never for a pat on the back. Jesus didn't stop doing good after only one leper came back to say thank you for healing him.[7] He didn't stop serving His Father when Peter denied Him three times[8] and Judas betrayed Him.[9] Of course, we are not Jesus by any stretch of the imagination. We crave and need affirmation. That's why encouraging one another is so important, it's imperative. A word of affirmation goes a long way and can stop the arrow of discouragement from taking root. The very word "discouragement" means to disconnect us from courage, and the word "encourage" means to inspire with courage. The accuser is always accusing, trying to make us throw in the towel, but when we encourage one another it shuts the accuser's mouth.

ANTIDOTE TO DIVERT SPIRITUAL DISASTER

One morning, I remember my husband, Michael waking up and telling me about a woman that was on his mind. She used to serve with him in the street ministry when we were at the Brooklyn Tabernacle. She had long since moved away, but he knew that he had her phone number written down somewhere. There was urgency in his spirit to call her, so before eating breakfast we turned the house upside down looking for this tiny piece of paper with this woman's phone number (this was before we had smartphones). When we finally found it, he called the woman and she began to tell him about how her husband had left her and their two little children. And because she was in great despair, she put poison in her drink and was about to serve it to herself and her children. The call from my husband had come in the nick of time.

The writer of Hebrews admonishes us to *"encourage one another daily, as long as it is called 'Today,' so that none of you may be hardened by sin's deceitfulness" (Hebrews 3:13, NIV)*. He is stating that there is a clear and present danger, a real possibility that on any given day, any given time, any one of us can become so discouraged that we may fall away by becoming hard hearted. We have no idea how a word of encouragement can give someone the strength to keep on keeping on by continuing to work hard for Him.

> The gift of encouragement is the antidote to avert spiritual disaster.

I plead with you, when the Holy Spirit quickens you to call or text someone, do it immediately. Do it "TODAY." I read somewhere, *"tomorrow is Satan's today."* That text or call could save someone's spiritual life. *The gift of encouragement is the antidote to avert spiritual disaster.* I oftentimes say that the gift of encouragement looks like Clark Kent but it really has Superman's power because it's able to rescue those from falling away, especially those who have become weary in doing well.

If Michael had waited until the next day to reach out to the woman, it would have been *Satan's today*. This woman is currently thriving in our church. God used a phone call to change her life. We tend to think that ministry is only done on platforms and in conferences, but the ministry of encouragement can be done everywhere, everyday, all day, when quickened by the Holy Spirit. When you reach out to someone you could be changing a life.

VISIBLE EVIDENCE OF OUR LOVE

Going back to our original text in Hebrews 6:10-12:

> God notices *how you have shown your love for Him by loving His people.* Wow, we show God how much we love Him by the way we care for His people, by the concern and devotion we show other believers or even non-believers. This means that we can't sing, "Jesus we love you" and not care for each other. How many believers do you know that don't like people? How many pastors complain about the people God has put under them to shepherd? We can't say we love God and not love His body. These two things are inseparable according to scripture. Jesus asked Peter, *"Do you love me?"* Peter answered, *"Yes Lord."* Jesus responded, *"Then feed my sheep."* Again the question was presented, *"Peter, do you love me?"* Peter answered, *"Yes Lord you know that I do."* Jesus responded, *"Feed my lambs."* Jesus was saying that you show me how much you love me by the way you nourish the people. Notice how Jesus said sheep and then lambs. This is a reference to both the young and old. We aren't to love one people

group more than another. The barometer by which I show God how much I love Him is indicated by the temperature at which I care for His people. God regards deeds of kindness done for his people as being done unto Himself. Matthew 25:35-40 states, *"I was hungry, and you fed me. I was thirsty, and you gave me a drink. I was a stranger, and you invited me into your home. I was naked, and you gave me clothing. I was sick, and you cared for me. I was in prison, and you visited me... whatever you did for one of the least of these brothers and sisters of mine, you did for me."* Isn't it strange in this day and age of ministry that these acts of kindness are seen as insignificant or minute, yet Jesus considers them as being the most important?

⌾ Then the writer of Hebrews tacks on the phrase, *"as you still do,"* which implies it's not a one-time act of kindness; it's continual caring. There are no limitations or boundaries by which we show our care and concern. Weekends aren't our days off. After all, God continues to love us and show concern for us each and every day and He never takes time off.

FINISHING WELL (STRONG)

⌾ *"Our great desire is that you will keep on loving others as long as life lasts"* (Hebrews 6:11a). There's an implication here that there is a great possibility that as we grow older in the Lord our care and concern for others might diminish, dwindle or cool down. The thrill is gone so to speak. Our hot passion for God has been interrupted by life's disappointments, weighing us down as our issues pile up and now this love-fest for God's people and ultimately for God takes a back seat to the pain of life. Weariness has set in! But the writer is saying, "despite the hurts, despite the weariness, keep on loving as long as life lasts." Despite the fact that you have been betrayed, lied about and are broken hearted, you've got to go the distance. There's no retirement when it comes to loving and caring for God's people. May we be found faithful to the end!

*   Lastly the scripture states, *"Then you will not become spiritually dull or indifferent."* This is our spiritual insurance policy. This is the attitude that keeps us safe. It prevents spiritual dullness and indifference. Here we see the direct link, the divine connection to remaining spiritually sharp. *It's loving people!* Staying connected to and loving people keeps us *Ageless!* For God so loved the world that He gave until He couldn't give anymore. According to the Greek, spiritual dullness and indifference has to do with the internal state of the heart. To be spiritually dull or indifferent is to go through the motions outwardly while being dead inwardly. It also means to become monotonous, unexciting. Still moving outwardly but with a loss of speed or momentum inwardly. Not moving with the same laser sharp focus that we once had on the inside. Spiritually lethargic. Just going thru the motions on autopilot. There's a loss of drive and enthusiasm. We've been neutralized. Still working, standing at our posts but dull to the things of the spirit. Dull to His voice. Somewhere along the way we have gotten exhausted in well doing. We unknowingly become dull and indifferent. Perhaps, somewhere along the way, we forgot that we are doing it for the Lord.

CHECK YOUR TEMPERATURE

If the enemy knows that God receives love by our care and concern for His people, and that it's our love for others that keeps us spiritually sharp and on our toes, doesn't it stand to reason that it would be his mission to destroy our unity and cause us to be indifferent to one another or to get us to stop loving one another? Once that happens, we will tend to keep our distance from one another, and soon we are serving God without the passion and power of the Holy Spirit. We become what the Bible refers to as "lukewarm." And being lukewarm is not an option. Bacteria grows in lukewarm places. You do know that God not only judges faithfulness, He also considers the temperature at which we work. We don't want to be those that are written about in Matthew 24:12 where it states in the end times, *"the love of many will grow cold."* He is speaking about believers, His very own body. We cannot allow the fiery darts of the enemy to put out our fire, as hard as he might try.

I pray that we would all remain steaming hot, because it's the fire of the Holy Spirit that will burn away the dullness and monotony. God's fire continually gives us the clarity and focus regarding why we do what we do. We need the continual fresh touch of God on our lives to give us an untiring, unwavering spirit. We absolutely need to keep encouraging each other. It is a mandate from God. Our hope is that we all finish strong. Our hope is that He says, *"Well done my good and faithful servant."* Remember God is not unjust. He sees all you have done for Him and all that you continue to do. He appreciates you!

AGELESS QUESTIONS

1. When was the last time you grew "weary in doing good?" How did that affect your care and concern for others?

_____

_____

_____

_____

_____

_____

_____

_____

_____

_____

_____

_____

_____

2. Which part of Hebrews 6:10-12 spoke to you the most? Explain.

_____

_____

_____

_____

_____

_____

_____

_____

_____

_____

_____

_____

_____

3. Do you consider yourself to be an encourager? Give an example that supports your answer.

_____

_____

_____

_____

_____

_____

_____

_____

_____

_____

_____

_____

_____

_____

4. How many years have you been serving the Lord? Have you noticed your levels of care and concern for others changing over the years? Explain.

_____

_____

_____

_____

_____

_____

_____

_____

_____

_____

_____

_____

_____

5. Have you taken your spiritual temperature lately? What does it read?

_____

_____

_____

_____

_____

_____

_____

_____

_____

_____

_____

_____

_____

CHAPTER FOUR

AGELESS = SALTY

"Salt is good for seasoning. But if it loses its flavor,
how do you make it salty again? You must have
the qualities of salt among yourselves and
live in peace with each other."

Mark 9:50

I F THERE IS one thing I enjoy, it's watching the Food
Network. I could sit in my comfortable chair and binge
watch shows like *Chopped*, *Beat Bobby Flay* and *Iron Chef*
all day. The competitions on these programs are so intense,
testing the talent of each chef until there is only one standing. These brilliant chefs are so creative, modernizing dishes
that have been popular favorites for years, elevating them to
a whole new level right before our eyes. The most stunning
thing to me is how many of the competitors are eliminated
for not using enough salt. The presentation of their recipe
is impeccable, the flavors are well balanced, and the food
is prepared to perfection, but the dish doesn't have the right
amount of salt! I'm always surprised when I hear the judge
say, "your dish lacks salt therefore we have to eliminate you."

The most basic of all ingredients disqualifies their dish from the competition. So often, salt is the only ingredient that can make the dish come alive.

The same is true with our lives. We can be creative, have great presentation, go to church and be involved, know the Greek and Hebrew, but if our lives have lost their saltiness how effective can we really be in a sin sick world? Salt is the only thing that sets every other "dish" apart. Too often we are more concerned about how our life looks on the outside instead of being concerned with what's really happening on the inside. Has the "salt" of our life lost its saltiness?

> The gift of encouragement is the antidote to avert spiritual disaster.

SALT IS THE SOLUTION

Years ago as I was returning home from a conference and before boarding my plane I stopped to get something to eat in this small greasy spoon diner. I was starving and cold and the only thing that sounded good was fried eggs and french fries. I know what you are thinking, "very healthy, Maria." I quickly thanked God for the food, grabbed one of the fries and quickly popped it in my mouth expecting warm, crunchy, salty potato perfection. It was tasteless and flat so I reached for the salt. I shook some on the fries and took another bite with great anticipation. But there was still no flavor. I thought, "Maybe I didn't shake enough on." So I shook and shook to no avail.

At first I couldn't grasp what was happening. There's *never* supposed to be a problem with the salt. That's the one ingredient that can salvage any meal. Salt is a fixer, making any meal come alive. But the salt wasn't salty. Unsalty salt, that's an oxymoron. Salt is supposed to be salty, it's called salt for a reason. The pepper was right next to the salt, but the truth is that there's no substitute for salt. Here I had in my hand a container that holds salt. A container that holds the contents within, but the content didn't coincide with the container. The content was flat and powerless to change the food.

So here's the lesson that I learned:

1. Although we place a major emphasis on packaging, in reality packaging isn't as important as the contents. I would rather have a plain box of salt than a fancy apparatus pretending to represent the contents inside. Likewise, I expect that people would rather have an encounter with a genuine believer, instead of someone who carries around a huge bible, has Christian bumper stickers on the back of their car, and speaks in "Christianese."

2. The outside label doesn't always coincide with the inner content. It's very sad when you come in contact with people who say they are believers, yet they are filled with hatred and un-forgiveness. It's what's on the inside that truly counts.

3. If something is dull, flat, old, or stale, shaking on more of it doesn't change the equation or the outcome. If you have found yourself stale and lifeless, stop continuing to go in the same direction. Ask the Holy Spirit to fill you with fresh life once again.

If you have
found yourself
stale and
lifeless, stop
continuing
to go in
the same
direction.

4. There's just no substitute for salt. There is no replacement for the fixer. Salty Christians are irreplaceable. Salt is the solution and lost people in this world are searching for the solution.

The religious people, or the Pharisees, in Jesus's day were His biggest headache. Their outer garments said, "I represent God," but the inside didn't coincide with the outside. The Pharisees studied about God but they didn't know the God that they so methodically studied. I believe they meant well, they thought that any kindness shown to an outsider was somehow betraying God, not realizing that God came for the outsider. He came to tear down barriers of religion, race, gender and class distinction and even forgive outright sin because of His shed blood.

Didn't they read how God covered Adam and Eve, forgave Abraham and Sarah and still gave them a son? He forgave Moses the murderer and turned him into a deliverer. And David the adulterer became known as a man after God's own heart. When Isaiah saw the Lord high and lifted up God saw that Isaiah was a man with unclean lips, yet God took the fire of heaven to cleanse his lips so He could use him as His mouthpiece. Because they cared more about the rules and their image, the Pharisees lost their ability to influence people to thirst for God. When they opened up their saltshaker, out poured self-righteousness, pettiness, jealousy, gossip, pride and racism. They had law without love, and religion without relationship. They became an exclusive religious club.

Jesus said that we are the *"salt of the earth,"* in Matthew 5:13. He didn't

> Jesus said that we are the *"salt of the earth,"* Matthew 5:13.

say that we are the pepper of the earth or the salt of the church. If we use all of our seasoning in the church pouring salt upon salt and then go out into the world (earth) our saltshaker will be depleted. Yet in order for our salt to really be effective it has to get out of the container and poured onto the unsalted earth. Our destination is the earth, the world that Jesus died for.

FACTS ABOUT SALT

1. Salt loses its flavor when it sits on the shelf, hidden away in its dark container for too long. It then becomes flat. If it's sitting in a cold damp place it becomes sticky. On the bottom of the box of salt in my pantry there is a "best used by" date. Just like the salt in my pantry, the salt of our life is only valuable if it is best used by our time on the earth. It is "best used by" when shaken out of the container onto the unsalted situations that we encounter every day. Salt has an expiration date. We are not the pepper of the earth. Pepper burns. Pepper is never digested. If they were to open us up when we go onto glory, if you consumed a lot of pepper there would be a sack filled with black pepper. The world cannot digest the Gospel when we shake out the wrong seasoning. It just sits on their insides undigested.

2. Salt creates thirst. Our lives are supposed to make people thirsty for the living God.

3. Salt is an influencer, an agent of change. We are to the earth what salt is to food.

4. Salt brings out the best in food and when used in proper proportions never overpowers it.

5. Salt is never the star of the dish. No one ever says, "I'll have a dish of salt please." However, when salt is used well, it makes every dish come alive.

6. Salt preserves, it kills bacteria, and stops the spread of corruption and decay. We are the earth's moral disinfectant. Jesus said, "*beware of the yeast of the Pharisees.*" When we are salted up, it keeps legalism in check.

7. Salt heals. In the ancient world they would place salt on wounds so they would close up and heal. We are called to bring healing to this world wounded by sin.

8. Bread baked without salt is shallow on the inside. In order to be whole we must be salted to perfection.

IS TOLERANCE COMPROMISE?

Our church, Christ Tabernacle, did a series entitled, "Questions for God." Week after week we tackled difficult subjects and sensitive issues. The question that I was assigned to teach on was no less challenging than that of my husband or son. "Is Tolerance Compromise?" If you were to have asked me that question forty-three years ago when I first got saved I would have said yes...a big fat *Yes!* I thought it was my job to set everybody straight. I would have been highly effective during the Crusades. Turn or burn! I would quickly whip an evangelism tract, filled with condemnation and guilt, out of my bag and hand it to any lost soul I'd meet. "You better get saved or you're going to a very hot, fiery place, and I don't mean Mexico mister," I'd threaten. Then I would be on my way—waving goodbye. God bless you. Jesus loves you! No love or kindness, all judgment and self-righteousness, very attractive and Christ-like. But for the grace of God, I'm not the same person I was four decades ago. When I took the plank out of my own eye that was blinding me from seeing how obnoxious I was, I was better able to help the one with the splinter in their eye. When I started to see all the mercy and grace that God had extended to me, it was sobering to realize how little I offered to others.

Tolerance is: Willing to exist with others who are different than you, while not necessarily agreeing with them. To clarify, in 1 Corinthians 5 the apostle Paul tells us not to tolerate known, repeated, unrepentant sin of a believer that is in our fellowship. Someone who claims to know Christ yet knowingly and continually keeps sinning without repenting. That should not be tolerated. We are not talking about believers. We are talking about living in the midst of non-believers, people that may be hostile to our beliefs.

Compromise is: Changing your views to appease others. Tolerance is *not* compromise. We must never change our views on biblical absolutes to appease anyone, *but* we should co-exist in a kind, respectful and loving way with our neighbors, co-workers, and family members that do not share our beliefs. Staying salty, so that we can be a good influence without compromising the truth of the Gospel.

As I was preparing to teach on the question I had been assigned, I felt as though the Holy Spirit flipped the question around on me. Instead of asking, is tolerance compromise? I felt Him say: "Is tolerance really God's best?" There are seminars on tolerance, teaching us how to tolerate or put up with those that are different than us, how to be "civil" with others. Tolerance may be the best the world has to offer, *but who wants to be tolerated?* I don't know about you, but I want to be loved and respected. I believe that is what every human being wants.

God offers something better...*unconditional love!* When we are not filled with God's amazing love we will simply tolerate people and in the process become short, curt and judgmental.

Tolerance can affect us at any age, from the young to the not so young and it can cause a disconnection in relationships. I think this is one of the main reasons for the so called "age barrier", which is another form of discrimination. If we are not careful tolerance can become a way of life, where we find ourselves merely tolerating our children and our parents that are now seniors.

> It is important to remember that the flesh tolerates but the spirit loves.

We may feel that their thoughts are not relevant and we lose the opportunity to learn from them. We forget that *"out of the mouths of babes"* found in Psalm 8:2; and that *"the gray hair of experience is the splendor of the old"* Proverbs 20:29b. It is important to remember that the flesh tolerates but the spirit loves. The more we grow spiritually the more we learn to love unconditionally.

In 2 Corinthians 5:20 the apostle Paul states, *"He has given us the ministry of reconciliation."* (ESV, paraphrased). The church is in the business of restoration, restoring the lost to Christ and Christ to the lost. God *so loved* the world, not *so tolerated* the world. His love is what made Him so influential. He made such a profound impact where tolerance and religion could have never penetrated. *Yet notice:* He never sacrificed truth for grace or grace for truth. He always had this delicate balance, this dance of grace and truth, and the only toes He ever stepped on were the religious, self-righteous critics. I believe Jesus was intolerant with them because they were

> God *so loved* the world, not *so tolerated* the world. His love is what made Him so influential.

so self-righteous that they refused to see themselves as they truly were. Blinded by their own faults, their mission was to point out people's flaws instead of reconciling them to God.

WHAT IS YOUR MISSION?

Think about the adulterous woman mentioned in the book of John. Jesus stands with her against all her religious accusers. He extends grace to her yet He doesn't compromise. That is fascinating. He asked her, *"Woman where are your accusers?"* He then proceeded to tell her, *"Neither do I [condemn you], go and sin no more"* (John 8:10b, 11b). He forgave her yet held her accountable. Colossians 4:6 (NIV) states, *"Let your conversation be always full of grace, seasoned with salt, so that you may know how to answer everyone."* Notice God's perfect order: Grace first. Salt second. In other words serve grace with salt, that's the divine recipe for sharing our faith. Otherwise they will get heartburn instead of a change of heart. John Knox said, "You can't antagonize and influence at the same time."[10] It is so important that we grasp this concept. Chris Hodges said, "Truth without grace is mean. Grace without truth is meaningless."[11] John 1:14 (NIV) states, *"Jesus was full of grace and truth."* I say, "Truth plus grace is meaningful."

There was a woman I used to counsel. She knew the Word and loved the Lord but knew little of God's grace. One day when we were meeting, she told me about a female co-worker

Notice God's perfect order: Grace first. Salt second. In other words serve grace with salt, that's the divine recipe for sharing our faith.

she had that was attracted to people of the same sex. The co-worker was not feminine and this repulsed the Christian woman. Although she never missed church on Sunday or a prayer meeting on Wednesday she had never connected the fact that Jesus loved sinners. She was on a self-righteous mission praying this woman out of the office or praying for her to get another job. When she would call or meet with me she would be seething with hatred all while believing she was on God's team. One day I said to her, "Why don't you invite this woman to lunch?" She responded, "Pardon me... lunch...Why would I ever want to do that?" In Matthew 5:50 it simply tells us to love God first and also love people. The two go hand in hand. I believe this woman had her saltshaker confused with the peppershaker.

> People don't need our commentary on their lives; they need the unconditional love of God.

The Bible is full of verses that clearly illustrate the mission of the church. 1 John 4:20 states, *"If we don't love people we can see, how can we love God, whom we cannot see?"* We can't say we love God, yet hate people that are different from us. People don't need our commentary on their lives; they need the unconditional love of God. They don't need us putting them down; they need God's hand extended through us, lifting them up. My son Jordan always says, "People don't care what we know unless they know that we care." Shouldn't there be a *connection* before there is a *correction*?

A member of our congregation shared a story with me about some churches that surrounded a gay nightclub in a particular area. When the people in the club would exit they were met with signs held up high, calling them hateful names and had judgmental fingers pointed at them. Another church in the area heard what was happening and they decided to dress up as angels and surround the nightclub. They put themselves in harms way to shield the gay men and women from the insults. A young gay man asked them, "Why would you do this for us?" The church said that the Holy Spirit wanted to let them know that God loved them. One man broke down and came to Christ right on the spot. Others started to weep. Walls started to come down. Romans 2:4 (NIV) reminds us, *"His kindness is intended to lead you to repentance."*

I counsel many women who after they get saved have deep issues with their families because they feel as though that person has betrayed them by leaving the family's religious affiliation. The newly saved people usually have a lot of zeal but are a bit short on wisdom. They start to tell the family members that they shouldn't pray to saints and statues, which is very true. But that is not the way to go about it. Didn't Jesus say in John 12:32, *"When I am lifted up from the earth, I will draw everyone to myself?"* So clearly the answer is not to put down the Blessed Mother Mary, or the Pope, or saints for that matter. *Just lift up Jesus!* He is the common, or should I say, the uncommon denominator in the situation. St Francis of Assisi said, "Preach the Gospel, and if necessary, use words."[12] 1 Peter 3:15 (NIV) states, *"Always be prepared to give an answer to everyone who asks you to give a reason for the hope you have. But do this with respect and gentleness."* Notice it says, *"Always be prepared to give an answer,"* which means that we must give people a chance to ask the necessary questions. Let them ask you, "What's different about you? Why aren't you fearful? Why don't you go out and party like everyone else?" Allow people to observe your life and then let them come to you to start the conversation.

TRUE STORY

My cousin Rose was about thirty years older than me, yet she never got married. She was a hat designer many years ago, for a top designer in New York City. When hats went out of style she taught herself how to use the computer and used her new skills to become a manager at a well-known brokerage firm on Wall Street. Rose had plenty of money. She lived on 6th Avenue in Greenwich Village. Her apartment had a sunken living room and she lacked for nothing, traveling to all four corners of the world. Although Rose had all the advantages of life she was a very bitter woman because she had had a long time affair with a married man who would not leave his wife. Even though Rose had this affair, she was very religious. And although she was religious she was a racist and a bigot, mean spirited and very proud. My family and I would invite Rose over to our house for the holidays because I was her only family. It wasn't easy to have her around. She would say things like "your church isn't a 'real' church" because it wasn't a particular denomination she approved of. She would say hateful things to me like, "do people really invite you to speak? Who would ever listen to you?" Sometimes Michael and I would go out to dinner with her in the city and I would think, "Lord I know I'm truly saved because you know and I know that I could easily push Rose in front of a moving bus and no one would be the wiser, except you Lord." That was the only thing that kept me in check. God would know! Needless to say, when it came to Rose I was full of pepper, showing her absolutely no grace.

As the years went by, Rose became sick with cancer. And being that I am the only family she had, I won the jackpot. I had to take care of Rose. That meant going into Manhattan several times a week, paying for parking in garages that are very expensive, going grocery shopping and cooking for her. I also took her to doctor appointments, picked up her medications and cleaned her apartment. She never gave me a dime. She would take out her wallet count her money in front of me and put the money back in her wallet. If I forgot my key to the downstairs door and had to ring the bell so she could buzz me in, she would scream through the intercom, "I'm not going to buzz you in for half an hour so you learn your lesson not to forget your key." Then she would call me a few choice words. As I waited for Rose to buzz me, I would call our church and speak with our receptionist Doreen so that she could pray for me. One day Doreen said with tears, "I believe the Holy Spirit wants to do a work in you." I couldn't imagine what work needed to be done; I was so busy admiring how perfect I was. I was doing all these things for Him, wasn't I? But it was Doreen's spirit filled words that led me to stop praying, "Lord change Rose" and start praying, "Lord change me." As long as I was merely *tolerating* Rose, I wasn't *loving* her. I went from barely putting up with Rose to having deep compassion for her. I was doing the exact same things but now it was with a different spirit. The Holy Spirit had filled me with His grace and salted me with God's love—*wow* what a difference. I no longer wanted to smother Rose with a pillow, but instead I was fluffing her pillows to make sure she was comfortable.

The last week of her life she asked me to pray that the Lord would take her home. She said, "I have a feeling that God answers your prayers." I asked her if she was ready to go home and she proudly answered, "Yes of course I'm ready." I proceeded to tell her that she wasn't going to get into heaven because she was white, rich or religious. I said, "Rose only one kind of person gets into heaven." She asked, "What kind of person is that?" I responded, "People who realize they are sinners in need of a Savior." I then asked, "Rose, are you a sinner?" She answered, "Yes" and she started to weep profusely. It was as though all the years of bitterness were washed away in but a few moments. She then prayed with me and for one whole week, Rose was the sweetest person alive. She passed onto glory with a smile on her face. I wish I had recognized my lack years earlier so I could have had a genuine loving relationship with Rose. She might have gotten saved so much sooner, relieved of all her bitterness and enjoyed the presence of the Lord while on this earth.

> We have a world that needs to be flavored with God's grace, mercy and kindness.

We have a world that needs to be flavored with God's grace, mercy and kindness. If you've become stale, it is imperative that you pour out all that has been bottled up on the inside so that He can fill up your container once again. We are all influencers, the agents of change that this world needs. Don't allow the spice of this world to replace the salt of the earth. And please remember not to keep all that goodness on the inside. Salt in the container doesn't do anyone any good. Show the world that God isn't who they think He is. Let's all shake out His goodness wherever we go!

AGELESS QUESTIONS

1. If you were asked the question, "Is tolerance compromise?" how would you have answered? After reading this chapter, has your answer changed? Explain.

_____

_____

_____

_____

_____

_____

_____

_____

_____

_____

_____

_____

_____

2. Explain in your own words what it means to be *"the salt of the earth."*

_____

_____

_____

_____

_____

_____

_____

_____

_____

_____

_____

_____

_____

3. After careful explanation, what seasoning do you use more of when dealing with people that are different with you— salt or pepper? Can you give an example?

_____

_____

_____

_____

_____

_____

_____

_____

_____

_____

_____

_____

_____

4. What do you think is the best way to test the condition of
   the salt in your life to see if it has lost its flavor?

_____

_____

_____

_____

_____

_____

_____

_____

_____

_____

_____

_____

_____

5. How does remaining "salty" keep us *Ageless*?

_____

_____

_____

_____

_____

_____

_____

_____

_____

_____

_____

_____

_____

CHAPTER FIVE

AGELESS = CONNECTED

"Instead, we were like young children among you.
Just as a nursing mother cares for her children,
so we cared for you. Because we loved you so much,
we were delighted to share with you not only
the gospel of God but our lives as well."

1 Thessalonians 2:7-8 (NIV)

MANY YEARS AGO my husband, Michael, was speaking at the Misfit Youth Conference that our son Chris headed up at the time through our church. That year there happened to be a gentleman in the audience from Zondervan, the book publishing company. After the service the gentleman approached my husband and I and said, "While you were speaking I noticed that there was something different about you. It has been my observation that the church at large has great speakers, leaders, even CEO's, but they are lacking fathers and mothers. You sir are a father and you ma'am are a mother." This gentleman had noticed that my husband was speaking from a parental position. Michael's gentleness, tenderness and sensitivity came through so much so that it brought this man to tears. What that gentleman had no idea of knowing is that the people in our church call us mom and dad even though we never asked them to. It was organic.

Shortly before that incident, my husband and I were being interviewed and were asked the question, "What is the one thing that you would want to be said about you when you leave this earth?" I thought to myself, "She looked good for her age, and she was a good mom, she loved God and His word." Simultaneously, Michael and I both said, "that we really loved the people." I have oftentimes said to other leaders, *"you will never be out of a job as long as you love the people."* Loving people is the ultimate privilege.

Loving people is the ultimate privilege.

I was recently listening to the radio when I heard an interview with an obstetrician. He said that since the Women's Movement, that started in the 1960's and blew up in the 1980's (and is still going strong), many women feel that having children is considered an impediment. He went on to share that children are looked at as an obstacle to a woman's professional progress, and that there has been a decline in working women having babies. Many women are getting married later in life and having babies in their late thirties and forties. But what stuck with me was when he mentioned the fact that these women who were having children later, were now asking, "Why anyone didn't ever tell them how wonderful having a baby was?" Are babies and children a lot of work? You bet they are. Do they interfere with your life plans? You bet they do!

But in my experience there has been no greater joy or sense of purpose than what my kids have given me. Unfortunately, because there has been such a huge emphasis on self as opposed to others, there has been a deep disconnect in this very important human need.

I also believe that culture has flowed into the Body of Christ. There are far too many people that come to church and leave immediately after service because they don't feel a need to connect. They don't want anyone to really know them or their business. This has even affected leadership. Over the years in ministry, I've noticed a trend towards leaders keeping their distance from their congregation often by being guarded and careful with how much they interact with their flock. Sadly, this has created an "us" and "them" mentality within the church, a society of "religious elite" if you will. This is contrary to God and the early church that shared everything. God takes pleasure in connecting with people just as a mother takes pleasure in connecting with her child. So it should be within the Body of Christ. As members of the body, we have the pleasure of seeing people come into the church one way and as we connect and share the power of God with them we witness the transformation, growth and metamorphoses that takes place in their life. Are there risks and hazards of the "job?" For sure, but the blessings far outweigh the risks!

In 1 Thessalonians 2:7-8 we see such a tender side to the Apostle Paul. He says he was as gentle as a breastfeeding mother among the Thessalonians. He paints a picture of intimacy, care and concern for those he was connected to. Notice, he doesn't compare himself to a father but rather a breastfeeding mother. Our Heavenly Father not only compares Himself to a mother wanting to gather her chicks (Matthew 23 and Luke 13) to keep them from danger, but in Isaiah 49:15 He says, *"Can a woman forget her nursing child? Can she feel no love for the child she has borne? But even if that were possible, I would not forget you!"* We know that there is a very slim chance of a breastfeeding mom forgetting to nourish her child, but even so—our Father is assuring us He will never forget us. Paul is comparing himself to a compassionate mother, not a preaching machine, theological commentator of truth, or a clever wordsmith (or as I like to put it a *swagilicious wordologist*). Not even close. He compared himself to a breastfeeding mother, one that gives sustenance through her very being. There is nothing and no

> There is nothing and no one that is as compassionate as a mother.

one that is as compassionate as a mother. The breastfeeding mother goes the distance. Everything about her is connected to her child. She is mindful of their every need. Likewise, our Heavenly Father is mindful of what we need, and so driven by compassion that He gave us His most precious gift, His very own son. He gave us a part of Himself. On top of providing us with the Ten Commandments, He also provided the grace we need to obey them. Paul, led by the Holy Spirit, didn't just meet the people and preach to them, giving them a ton of doctrinal truths, but he gave them his very life.

In the scriptures the analogy of breastfeeding and even breasts were oftentimes used as a symbol for spiritual growth. In Song of Songs 8:8-9 (NIV) it says, *"We have a little sister, and her breasts are not yet grown. What shall we do for our sister on the day she is spoken for? If she is a wall, we will build towers of silver on her. If she is a door, we will enclose her with panels of cedar."* It's the older sisters speaking about the younger sister. They're not gossiping about her, but rather, trying to come up with a plan that can help her develop into the woman of God she was created to be. They are not criticizing nor scrutinizing her. They first say if she is a door, symbolizing danger, harm, vulnerability, open to everyone, then we need to come up with a plan to protect her. They go on to say, if she is a wall, symbolizing protection and strength, formidable and able to stand on her own, then we can build towers of silver on her. In other words, we can celebrate her and use her as a godly standard for all to see because her life is bringing glory to God. Song of Songs 8:10 (NIV) goes on to say, *"I am a wall, and my breasts are like towers. Thus I have become in his eyes like one bringing contentment."* It's like the older sister is saying, *"I'm mature and my breasts are a DD in the spirit, but my sister is still in a training bra. She's a AA."* I believe they realized that because they are connected to the Bridegroom, they are also connected to those whom He loves. There is ownership and attachment, a divine connection so to speak. Though Paul was never a parent in the natural, scriptures shows he had many spiritual children. He learned to be tender because he realized how tender God was with him.

When I think of a breastfeeding mother the following things come to mind:

- Sacrifice
- Commitment
- Willingness to constantly pour out
- Emptying oneself so someone else can be nourished
- Patience
- Complete connection
- Always available
- Total inconvenience
- Invasion of your time and life
- Willingness to have your body image altered

The definition of sacrifice is to give up something you love for something you love even more. Motherhood is an example of offering your body as a living sacrifice. Mothers give up their time, treasures and talents for something they love even more, their children

The church at large has moved out of the birthing room, the place of sacrifice. Where are the midwives, mothers, fathers and mentors? Those that would go the distance until they saw Christ formed in someone else's life. Those that would carry someone else's burden, that stood in proxy as a surrogate. Unfortunately many churches have turned into cosmetic surgery centers or luxury spas. Aren't we supposed to be Holy Ghost hospitals? We now come to church for a little nip and tuck, a little injection of collagen or a little lift. We've become more concerned about receiving a blessing than being a blessing. If the pastor doesn't make us feel good about ourselves and massage our aches and pains we leave and find another church where we can get a temporary fix from what ails us. The truth is we are short changing ourselves from experiencing the fullness of what God offers through being connected in community with others.

The Bible instructs those who are older in the Lord, not necessarily old in age, to teach the younger (Titus 2:3). This is not a suggestion but a command. Remember, there is always someone younger than you in the faith. Seasoned women, and dare I say seasoned men, who have gone through some stuff, have walked through the valley of the shallow of death and are still standing strong should be willing to teach the younger. That means we are to:

- Nurture
- Mentor

🖊 Empower

🖊 Breathe life into the not so seasoned

🖊 Teach them how to stand, pray, believe and not faint.

BREASTFEEDING FACTS

Spiritual Breastfeeding is God's insurance policy that we remain accountable and connected to one another. I once heard a woman say: *"There's something so right about a system that makes one human responsible for another."* The same is true in the Body of Christ: as we receive, we are to give back out. As we empty out, we are to get filled up again. The spiritual cycle of life is only active as we are imparting life. Breastfeeding moms are fearless, selfless, and shameless in an effort to impart life to their children and continue the cycle of life. They whip out their breasts whenever and wherever for the sake of a crying baby. It's not a chore to them.

I've discovered several ways in which breastfeeding correlates to our spiritual lives:

Fact #1: An inter-dependent relationship is formed.

The baby needs what the mother can supply, but the mother has to choose to release it to the baby, otherwise both would experience pain and loss. They are inter-dependent; they're connected in close proximity. Their bond causes both to yearn for one another. Much like us in our spiritual walk, the mother has to be mindful of what she takes in because it in turn affects her output of what nourishes her child. Scripture warns us to watch what we digest, what we listen to, and what we talk about. Proverbs 14:1 states, *"A wise woman builds her home, but a foolish woman tears it down with her own hands."*

Forming inter-dependent relationships in the kingdom help us because not only is the younger Christian blessed, the older Christian has tremendous joy in seeing them grow stronger. You could be exhausted when you walk into church, but when you see people transformed from the challenges of life it all becomes worth it. Your joy is attached to their success. 1 Thessalonians 3:7-9 (NIV) states, *"Therefore, brothers and sisters, in all our distress and persecution we were encouraged about you because of your faith. For now we really live, since you are standing firm in the Lord. How can we thank God enough for you in return for all the joy we have in the presence of our God because of you?"* Paul was having a "glory fit" in prison because the people he loved were standing firm in the faith. His joy was always connected to someone else's success. (Joy = Jesus, others, and you.) In other words, if you're doing well then I'm doing well. That's the secret to "joy unspeakable and full of glory." Isn't that how a healthy parent feels? If her child is not well then she is not well. Paul's joy had nothing to do with his circumstances. It was connected to the success of the people he had nursed at his spiritual breasts.

Ageless means being productive and effective in the lives of others. What does that look like?

- Love one another as you have been loved. (John 13:34)

- Comfort one another, as you have been comforted. (2 Corinthians 1:4)

- "Give and it shall be given," means to give as freely as you have received (see Matthew 10:8).

- As we refresh others we ourselves will be refreshed. (Proverbs 11:25)

Ageless means being productive and effective in the lives of others.

"I pray that you would be active in the activity of sharing your faith, then you will know what God's will is?" Philemon 1:6 (KJV, paraphrased)

It's only in the activity of sharing your faith that you will know what God's will is. The bottom line is this: If you want to be blessed, be a blessing.

Fact #2: When you breastfeed you become stronger.

I heard when a mother breastfeeds her uterus becomes stronger and she is able to hold more children. The same is true spiritually, as we pour out to others what we've gained in the Spirit, our inner man is strengthened and we will be able to pour out on more "spiritual children." You may start by mentoring one person, but before you know it, you gain the strength to mentor and mother more and more. As you begin the process, mentoring may start by merely sending a text when you feel quickened by the Holy Spirit. It can be as simple as letting someone know you are thinking of and praying for them, or inquiring about how they are doing. As you see the fruit from your obedience you will be able to spread your wings and reach out more and more.

Fact #3: The more you breastfeed the more milk your body makes.

When a new mom starts the process of breastfeeding I'm sure she wonders if she'll have what it takes to go the distance. But it's in the subtraction that there is addition. The same can be said for us in regards to spiritual mentoring relationships; we are fearful that we don't have what it takes. But we simply have to give out what we have. In God's Word He instructs us to open our mouth and He will fill it, open our heart and He will give us rivers of compassion. Unless we "expel" what we do have there will never be an increase.

Consider the widow in 2 Kings 4, the prophet asked her, *"What do you have in the house?"* She replied, *"Nothing at all, except a flask of olive oil."* Literally this meant "one" anointing of oil for me. But the prophet said, *"Borrow as many empty jars as you can from your friends and neighbors. Then go into your house…"* The prophet's answer to her lack was finding vessels emptier than herself and pouring into them the little she possessed. Go into your house (bring them close to you) and start pouring that oil out. Notice oil produced oil as she replicated what she had. Whatever she poured out she was filled up with the same. When she stopped collecting jars the oil stopped flowing. God doesn't waste His anointing; it's meant to be given away.

Fact #4: In order to breastfeed you've got to take your shirt off.

Breastfeeding requires you to be naked, transparent and vulnerable with skin-to-skin contact. When we consider doing this with others, fear says: you have to appear perfect, don't let them see your imperfections, like your cellulite, lumps and bumps leading us to believe that what we have isn't enough. But your baby doesn't see the imperfections. The biggest hurdle is accepting that we do have something to give and then taking the obedient step of responsibility to give it out.

Fact #5: There might be pain or injury along the way.

One hazard of breastfeeding is that your nipples might get sore and chapped, causing them to bleed and therefore need salve to heal. Anytime we engage in honest relationship, there too could be pain or hurt feelings. But because of Jesus, we can anoint ourselves and keep on going. Other times moms may develop *mastitis*, a serious infection in the tissue around the breast. When this happens, the mother is urged to breast-feed despite the pain because the breast milk is not affected. If the mom stops her ducts will clog up leading to an abscess and requiring surgical draining. It's better for the mom to push through the pain in order to avoid the knife and scarring. Chances are, when you reach out to others you may get bit, which can make us bitter. When that happens we put our shirt back on, button up and swear off reaching out because we don't want to be hurt again. But if your baby bites you, you don't ring your neighbor's doorbell and ask her to care for your baby. We need to ask God for the resilience to go the distance, instead of leaving it to others.

Fact #6: Stopping leads to drought.

The sure fire way to have your milk dry up is to stop or slow your breastfeeding. If we stop connecting and trusting people, we will isolate and grow cynical and bitter. That's a pain much greater to bear than being bit. I encourage you not to take the coward's way out. Let's be fearless, shameless and selfless.

There are three kinds of people that are reading this book right now:

1. People who have pushed through the pain.

2. People who have buttoned up and shut down.

3. People who haven't even started the process of breastfeeding because they don't think they have much to give.

The Holy Spirit
wants you
to know that
you have
greatness
on the inside
waiting to
overflow out
of you.

The Holy Spirit wants you to know that you have greatness on the inside waiting to overflow out of you. Take off the lid of fear and fan into flame the gift of God within you. Don't let that greatness lie dormant, for God has not given us a spirit of fear. He gave us a Spirit of fearlessness and it's full of power, ability to love and a mind that has its priorities straight!

This is what is required to be productive and effective or *Ageless*. We have to let the Holy Spirit press us, and when we do, we will be surprised to see what comes out. Let's not live lonely, let's live loving – *you're not living unless you're giving!*

THE BODY OF CHRIST

"Take this baby and nurse him for me, and I will pay you" Exodus 2:9 (NIV).

We know that this scripture comes from the story of Moses' mother being told by Pharaoh's daughter to breastfeed Moses, which unbeknownst to her was her very own son. So she not only gets the benefit of looking into this babies eyes while holding him close. She gets the opportunity to feed him from what's within her, while watching the baby transform and grow right before her eyes. Bonus time...she gets paid to boot! We know that even though Moses grew up in a totally different culture, he never forgot the closeness and love he felt from being nourished by his mother's breast milk. His mother saw up close and personal that he was no ordinary child yet she had no idea that he would be the deliverer for her and all her people. God chose them both to be a part of His divine plan.

Isn't that how it is in the body of Christ? We get the most amazing opportunity to bring the brand new wide-eyed baby, freshly born again, close to us where they can drink from our life's experiences. We can pour into them the pure milk of God's word. Yet we have no idea the potential that's inside of them and what they will end up looking like but we get to be a part of this divine process. We get to shape their diet, giving them the lowdown, influencing them on what fountain to drink from and what fountain to avoid. How cool is that? Like Moses's mother who took what she had, a simple basket, rubbed it with tar and pitch making it into an arc of safety. When she placed him in the dangerous water of the Nile, he would not drown or be eaten alive by filthy insects and predators.

We were once those babies who were protected and nourished by simple people who cared enough about us to take what they had and use it for our benefit. Someone who saw our potential. Someone who prayed for us knowing how dangerous the world is covered us in prayer so we didn't have to drown.

Now as we stand straight and tall we are able to pull others up to higher ground. As we take them to our spiritual breast we are able to impart life, strength and wisdom stored up from years of experience and abiding in the presence of the Lord. We not only get to experience this precious connection, we get a reward from the Lord! *Wow!* Our labor is not in vain. God sees and pays us back. Our life is enriched and when we see the potential come to life of the one we have nourished, we know we had a big part to play in their growth and development. No one repays us like the Lord and there's no greater reward from seeing your knowledge and experiences passed down to someone else. So don't be afraid!

You are probably thinking, how could I connect? What do I have in common with someone not my age? Well I have two things to say about that:

1. Just remember...go back to how you felt. All the questions you had in the beginning of your journey. The fears you had. Were you going to make it through those treacherous trials and those fiery temptations? I know you wish you could forget about them but they are a valuable commodity. Let those trials pay you dividends. Get a lot of mileage out of them! Didn't you appreciate the elder that held your hand and took time to teach you scripture and encouraged you to hold on? Didn't you appreciate the phone call or the lunch date? We are all the same on the inside even though our outward style changes. We all have the same needs. We need one another!

2. We have the Holy Spirit! Every born again believer has been given the Holy Spirit and He is our connection to all things spiritual and He is our connector to one another. He is the ancient of days and never changes. But don't forget He makes all things new. He speaks the same language to every one of us, on the inside, in the deepest recesses of our hearts where we can communicate our deepest needs and fears to one another on a spiritual level.

We have so much more in common than we realize. Let's connect with one another and allow the connector to iron out the details.

AGELESS QUESTIONS

1. In your personal life were you blessed with having a mentor or spiritual parent to help you along your faith journey? Explain how that relationship (or lack of relationship) affected your spiritual growth.

---

2. Were you or are you a breastfeeding mom? Share your physical experience and correlate it to a spiritual experience.

_____

_____

_____

_____

_____

_____

_____

_____

_____

_____

_____

_____

_____

_____

3. I mentioned three types of people in this chapter. Which one do you relate to and why?

_____

_____

_____

_____

_____

_____

_____

_____

_____

_____

_____

_____

_____

_____

AGELESS

4. Write out Song of Songs 7:7 (NIV) and translate how that
   might apply to you.

_____

_____

_____

_____

_____

_____

_____

_____

_____

_____

_____

_____

_____

_____

5. Read 2 Thessalonians 2:7-12. In this passage of scripture Paul refers to children, nursing mothers and fathers. Write out in your own words the role and responsibility of each people group.

_____

_____

_____

_____

_____

_____

_____

_____

_____

_____

_____

_____

_____

6. List at least three reasons why a person would not want to
   be a breastfeeding mother.

_____

_____

_____

_____

_____

_____

_____

_____

_____

_____

_____

_____

CHAPTER SIX

AGELESS = GRATEFUL

"Carefully determine what pleases the Lord."

Ephesians 5:10

D O YOU REMEMBER the undying devotion you had when you first gave your life to Christ? No task was too difficult, no mountain too high to keep us from wanting to please Him. As Ephesians 5:10 states, this should always be our goal. We were so grateful that God the Father sent Jesus, His one and only Son to save sinners such as us. Gratitude is what drove us to please Him. I can remember the day when, as a believer, nothing would keep me out of a service that was saturated with the Presence of the Lord. We gave and gave until we had no more to give. Women would have their babies and the next week they would be back in fellowship with their babies wrapped up tightly on the pew next to them. We didn't think about germs then or if the babies had their shots. We somehow knew the best place for the baby and the parent was in God's presence. I know this is not politically correct nowadays, but I say all this to paint the image of desperate people who were desperate for God. Sold out and deliriously out of our minds filled with gratitude that made them Kingdom minded. We know that even Mary brought Jesus to the temple when He was 8 days old. But times have changed from the days where we would never think to miss a prayer meeting, never factoring in how cold or hot it was. We needed God and we needed each other. Somehow Christianity has become more about what we can get than what we can give. We have subtly become self-absorbed, calculating what I can and cannot do for God and if and when I can come to church or not. A sense of entitlement has moved us away from being grateful.

AN ATTITUDE OF GRATITUDE

The Merriam-Webster definition of gratitude is the state of being grateful or thankful. The synonym is appreciative.[13] Gratitude is a virtue. Cicero, the Greek philosopher, said, *"not only is gratitude the greatest of all virtues but it is the parent of all."*[14] I am one of the most grateful people alive. I have been saved for forty-two years and I still can't believe that God allows me to worship Him. You see I was a terrible sinner, selfish and self-centered. But Jesus chose to save me so everything I now do I do for Him. A worship leader recently asked me for a thirty second definition of what I considered "ministry" to be. I explained to him that the word "minister" simply means "servant" therefore ministry is service. Everything I do is ministry. Whether I'm mopping the floor, cooking for my family, babysitting grandchildren, connecting with people or speaking at a conference, to me it's all ministry because *it's all about Him!* Every one of those things is an opportunity to allow the love of God to flow out of us if we remember how much we are loved. You might ask how can mopping a floor be ministry? When you do it with a grateful heart, thanking God that you have a floor to mop, it becomes an opportunity to love on God.

Ministry is so much more than a platform or a title. God has given me incredible opportunities to travel and share His word. Wherever I go I can tell a lot about the church to which I'm headed long before I get into the building. It has nothing to do with whether the church is rich, poor, large or small. It has nothing to do with the type of restaurant they take me to. I've had some of the warmest fellowship at IHOP. It has everything to do with the posture of their heart. Some people pick me up at the airport and they make me feel like *they have to do this*, it's their duty. Others make me feel like *they get to do this!* They carry around with them what I call an attitude of gratitude. That attitude transfers into the way they serve the Lord on every level. Grateful people are generous people. He who has been forgiven much loves much (see Luke 7:47). It's the overflow of appreciation for what He has already done. It's impossible to be over the top wholeheartedly in love with Jesus and also be calculated and cautious. We can't be stingy and passionate at the same time. Paul says in 2 Corinthians 5:14 (NIV), *"For Christ's love compels me."* It drives me and thrusts me and launches me to do things that I would not naturally do. I don't know about you but there are times I'm compelled to bless somebody. I've got to encourage, pray, cook, and give otherwise I would lose my mind.

> Ministry is so much more than a platform or a title.

TRUE STORY

One day my assistant, Penny, received a call with an invitation for me to come speak at a conference. The conference was scheduled to run Monday through Thursday and I would be speaking a total of four times. After I had accepted the invitation, they called back and asked if I could come two days earlier to speak at their Sunday service in advance of the conference. I accepted. They booked the plane tickets and instead of a direct flight they chose one that included a three-hour layover. A trip that should have taken a total of five hours (including the 2 hour early arrival at the airport) took ten hours, all to save a little money. Once Penny and I finally arrived, there was no one waiting for us at the airport. Someone showed up to retrieve us over an hour later, apologized for getting there late and helped us into their filthy van. Due to traffic, a drive that should have taken one and a half hours took three hours. We arrived at the hotel tired and hungry, and the driver pulls up, takes out our luggage (which we wheel to the front desk), and says, "take this" as he places a case of water into my arms and piles on a box of saltine crackers. In all fairness, my speaker agreement does request water and crackers, but it's more of a precautionary measure. He then drives away.

This was a prelude of things to come. The hotel was under renovation so there was the smell of cigarettes in the rooms that had been used for smokers in the past. Everything was dingy and sticky and of course there was no restaurant on the premises. The van we rode in from the airport was cleaner than the hotel room. On Sunday morning we arrive to this gorgeous church. They had a café, so I hurried to pick up two coffees and muffins for us. The woman behind the counter asked me for $6.00, as she had no idea I was their guest speaker. That morning I spoke in two of their worship services. The people were more reserved than warm, and not what I would consider generous with their worship. After service the pastor took us for brunch at the Country Club to which he belonged, along with his family and some staff. They dropped us off at the hotel that Sunday afternoon and never came back until Monday evening for the conference. *We were starving.* I remembered the café so I rushed in before the service and ordered two coffees and two muffins. The associate pastor's wife, who ran the café and had come to brunch with us the previous day, greeted me and then proceeded to ask for $6.00. I swallowed hard and reached down for my wallet. After the service the associate pastor asked if we were hungry. I thought to myself, *"Do birds fly, or fish swim?"* We hadn't eaten a meal since yesterday's brunch. We got into the back of his Cadillac and he took us to a Burger King drive thru. Penny and I ordered a cheeseburger meal. No Super Size meal...we didn't want to be greedy. He then turned to us and asked for the money. I was in utter disbelief. I felt so humiliated. I reached into my wallet and handed him enough money to buy him a meal also. He took it. By the end of the week I had ministered six times. I also discovered that other speakers for the conference were put in the renovated part of the hotel. I was perplexed. Was it because I was a woman? Was it because I wasn't part of their denomination? Or was it God wanting to give me this illustration?

A TALE OF TWO HEARTS

The last night, as I opened the door to my hotel room a gigantic water bug crawled out. I shut the door to my room and wept not only for myself but for my assistant Penny as well. The Holy Spirit prompted me to read Luke 7. My eyes fell down to the story about the way a religious leader hosted Jesus. I began to see that it was an awful experience. How dare this Pharisee, this prominent leader in the synagogue, treat Jesus in this fashion? As I read the story I saw it in a whole new light. The story is really a comparative narrative. It's a tale of two hearts.

- One was a religious man—a temple goer, tassel wearing, Torah reading elder. The other didn't have the proper attire.

- One was well versed in scripture. The other wasn't a bible scholar by any means.

- One was respectable of good reputation. The other was not so good.

- One had a secure position. The other had just quit their job.

- One gave Jesus nothing but an invitation to his home. The other wasn't on the guest list but decided to crash the party.

- One was calculated. The other refused to put a price tag on what was priceless.

- One was looking to impress the masses. The other was performing for an audience of one.

To provide you with some background: Jesus's ministry was blowing up. He was the man of the hour. This religious man wanted to capitalize on Jesus' fame. So he invites Jesus to his house for dinner. Having Jesus in his home drew a crowd and made him look and feel important. Parties in those days were a public event. The uninvited guests could stand on the perimeter and observe the guests from afar. Sort of like standing on the sidelines watching the "who's who" of Hollywood walk the Red Carpet. The religious man had no intention of really giving Jesus a "place of honor" in his house. He just wanted to use His name. After all, He was the inviter, while Jesus was the invitee. Therefore, he was in charge of how much he wanted to give and how much he didn't. How much affection he wanted to pour out and how much he didn't.

This is kind of like us, we invite Jesus into our hearts therefore we are in charge! It's my house and I decide how much I want of Jesus and how much I don't. How much I want to give and how much I don't. Of course I invite Him to dinner, after all I need him to bless the food.

The religious man didn't "feel like" extending himself to Jesus that day. He wasn't in a generous mood. Imagine the King of Kings, the resurrected Christ, is subject to our moods. He doesn't even give Jesus the bare minimum. No water to wash His feet, which was common courtesy. No kiss of welcome, which was customary. A kiss would have meant honor, affirmation, and acknowledgement. He basically gave Jesus the cold shoulder. That was the equivalent to being inside the house but left holding your coat. No oil to anoint His head—that was reserved for the guest of honor, oil meant value. He didn't even treat Jesus as an equal.

What this man didn't do spoke volumes. He gave the bare minimum. He gave minimal hospitality but had maximum opinion. God had to use an outsider to show up the insider.

I know the chapter heading reads, "The Sinful Woman." I believe it should read, "The Grateful Woman" who used to be sinful just a few days ago, but now she is forgiven. She somehow hears through the grapevine that Jesus is going to be at 666 Cemetery Lane. She cannot contain herself, determined to bless Him somehow, when she realizes that she owns this valuable alabaster jar worth a year's wages. This was her nest egg, her 401K, and she had just quit her job. But none of those things matter. She starts running toward the house with tears involuntarily flowing down her cheeks, she comes from behind and collapses at His feet, the feet that walked out of His way to bring her the Good News. Her tears provide the much-needed water that was not provided for Him, but she doesn't know that. Did she notice the streaks of dirt caused by her tears and wonder why was He deprived of having His feet washed? This was unthinkable. She can't leave his feet wet, but she doesn't have a towel and no one is offering her one. All they were offering at the moment were cold stares of unbelief. After all, her kind of people, uninvited no less, were not supposed to be in the home of a holy religious leader. The only thing in her possession that she could wipe his feet with was her clean, beautiful, long hair.

> Worship isn't worship unless it costs you something.

She does whatever it takes to clean the feet of the One who cleaned her life. Then she kisses them all without her knowing she's providing the kiss that they failed to give Him. She could have stopped there, but she knew that wouldn't be enough. Worship isn't worship unless it costs you something. The tears and the kiss are the prelude. Giving consummates the act. She takes the lid off and anoints His feet with the costly ointment in her alabaster jar. She has no clue that this act makes up for the oil that was withheld. She poured and poured until her jar was empty. She's now financially depleted but ironically she's the richest person in that room. Jesus hits the nail on the head when He said, *"I tell you, her sins—and they are many—have been forgiven, so she has shown me much love. But a person who is forgiven little shows only a little love"* (Luke 7:47). It's really the one who realizes the depth of their own sin and the greatness of His mercy that will love as this woman loved. Notice He equates her generous action with the proportion of her gratitude.

THE RIPPLE OF GRATITUDE

One day a woman named Judy Little called my assistant, Penny, and asked if I would come speak for five people in Canada. She had seen me on a Christian TV program there and decided to reach out. Penny replied, *"If it's the Lord's will, I know Maria will go."* She called back the next week and asked if I would come for ten people. Penny gave her the same reply. The next week she called again and asked if I would come for twenty people. I said *absolutely yes!* Her persistence was very endearing to me. Little did we know that Judy suffered from Multiple Sclerosis, requiring her to be in a wheelchair, so she had her eighty-five year old father pick us up from the airport.

Judy Little had been saved about two years prior, and she was so grateful for her salvation that she wanted everyone to know this Jesus. Her husband had left her, she didn't have much money, but she had holy zeal with no limits, and no boundaries. When she extended the invitation for me to come speak, she called every radio station in the area and her persistence convinced them to give her free airtime to promote the event. She also contacted every local church, whether it be Catholic, Episcopalian, Presbyterian, Pentecostal, Baptist, and Seventh Day Adventist, and sent them an Internet link for the episode of 100 Huntley Street, the Christian TV program on which she had seen me. The response was so overwhelming she had to rent out a reception hall. Judy didn't have access to a worship band, so her son's band learned *Amazing Grace*. Over 1,000 people showed up that night, and hundreds came to know the Lord all because Judy Little was *so grateful*!

THE AGELESS BENEFITS
OF GRATITUDE

Imagine what our lives would look like if we maintained an *attitude of gratitude*. The benefits of gratitude are endless, or should I say *Ageless* and affect every area of our lives (mind, body, soul). It's important to realize that gratitude is not positive thinking; it is being thankful or appreciative of the gift of life that God has given to us. The awareness of what God has done for mankind and for each of us individually gives us the power to live above our circumstances.

Research has proven that gratitude is essential for happiness, but modern times have regressed gratitude into a mere feeling rather than retaining its historic value, a virtue that leads to action.[15] Judy Little's gratitude led to action. She went above and beyond the call of duty and took bold courageous steps to share with others what Christ had done for her. Even in the midst of her personal struggles both physically and emotionally she was able to look at all that she gained instead

Gratitude is not positive thinking; it is being thankful or appreciative of the gift of life that God has given to us.

of all that she lost. Why has the level of devotion changed in the lives of so many believers? I think one major cause is that the *attitude of entitlement* has replaced the *attitude of gratitude*. I recently read an article in Greater Good Magazine online that said, "Entitlement is at the core of narcissism. This attitude says, 'Life owes me something,' or "People owe me something" or "I deserve this."[16] Entitlement and self-absorption are massive impediments to gratitude. Entitlement will hinder our level of devotion and cause us to become disconnected from the very purpose of the church.

AGELESS QUESTIONS

1. Have you maintained your level of devotion to the Lord from when you first got saved? _____ Yes _____ No

2. If your answer is No, can you describe what has changed (i.e. church attendance, serving in ministry, concern for others) and why it has changed?

_____

_____

_____

_____

_____

_____

_____

_____

_____

_____

3. In your own words explain what an *attitude of gratitude* looks like.

_____

_____

_____

_____

_____

4. Would you consider yourself being forgiven of much?

_____ Yes _____ No

5. Depending on the answer to the previous question, how does that play out in your everyday life?

_____

_____

_____

_____

_____

6. Write out Luke 7:40-42. Explain in your own words how
   forgiveness and *gratitude* are linked together.

_____

_____

_____

_____

_____

_____

_____

_____

_____

_____

_____

_____

_____

_____

7. As you have gotten older do you find yourself more able to appreciate the people, events and situations that have been part of your life history? Explain.

_____

_____

_____

_____

_____

_____

_____

_____

_____

_____

_____

_____

_____

CHAPTER SEVEN

AGELESS = SELFLESS

"Just as water mirrors your face,
so your face mirrors your heart."

Proverbs 27:19 (MSG)

C HRISTIANITY BY DEFINITION means Christ-likeness and to be Christ like is the epitome of selflessness. Somehow Christianity has become more about what we can receive instead of what we can give. It's become all about our purpose, our process, and our potential, but the most fruitful people were those who rarely focused on themselves. They were kingdom minded, more concerned about building God's house than their own. They were the real heroes of the faith, the ones who moved heaven's cause forward.

In the book of Exodus we find unlikely heroes using unlikely things to build up the kingdom of God. Women who were kingdom minded. They were not allowed to go past the Tent of Meeting yet they were instrumental in providing a key piece of furniture needed inside of God's house. God desperately wanted to live amongst His people and He made a request.

Somehow
Christianity
has become
more about
what we
can receive
instead of
what we
can give.

A SACRED RESIDENCE

"I want the people of Israel to build me a Sacred Residence where I can live among them. You must make the Tabernacle and its furnishings exactly according to the plans I will show you" (Exodus 25:8, paraphrased).

These women were intricately involved in fulfilling this request. This story is found in Exodus 38:8 (NKJV, *paraphrased*), *"He* (Bezalel the chief craftsman of the tabernacle) *made the laver* (sacred wash basin) *of bronze and its base of bronze from the bronze mirrors of the serving women who assembled at the door of the Tabernacle of Meeting* (or the door of the Tent of Meeting)." Not to be confused with the Tabernacle. Let me unpack this for you. The Tent of Meeting was a prelude to the Tabernacle. It was provisional, accepted at the present time but likely to be changed. The Tent of Meeting had none of the Tabernacle furnishings but it did have God's presence.

To understand the background for why there was a Tent of Meeting we have to go to Exodus 33:7a (NKJV, *paraphrased*) where it states, *"Moses took his tent* (remember they were in the wilderness and dwelt in tents) *and pitched it outside of the camp, far from the camp, and called it the tabernacle of meeting* (or tent of meeting)." Tabernacle means: residence or dwelling place, resting place. It was the portable dwelling place of God amongst His people. In Exodus 33:9 (NKJV) it goes on to say, *"When Moses entered the tabernacle, that the pillar of cloud descended and stood at the door of the tabernacle, and the Lord talked with Moses."*

SYMBOLIC PICTURE

Before there was a tabernacle building there was a tent that was portable. Once the tabernacle was built it became stationery. As the people of God who carry His presence, we are now the portable tents, and the local church is the stationery place where God's people gather. Just as Moses said in Exodus 33:15 (NIV), *"If your Presence doesn't go with us, do not send us up from here."* We should want to be carriers of His Presence, representative of the seal of the Holy Spirit. Notice that Moses pitched "his" tent, which represents a personal investment, a far enough distance away so he could hear from God. Away from the noise and influence of other voices. This was his quiet time. Exodus 33:7b (NKJV) continues, *"And it came to pass that everyone who sought the Lord went out to the tabernacle of meeting which was outside the camp."* People knew that Moses was with God. When you carry the presence of God people are drawn to you.

Going back to the original text in Exodus 38:8 we notice that this verse tells us that there were women that assembled at the door of the tent. Women of all ages, all stages, God-seekers that would gather to serve the Lord. The word "serving" used here is the Hebrew word Tsaba', which means: to wage war, to war in warfare, to go forth as a troop as an organized army.[17] These women were worshippers that were battle ready. This verse could easily read "warring women" instead of "serving women" who assembled at the door of the tent. One of the things that made these women different is that they were ex-slaves or servants of Egyptian households. While they were now free, they chose to be servants of God, to be warring women. Keep in mind that, as women, they weren't allowed inside. The door was closed to them. But they didn't allow the closed door to make them bitter because they knew they had access to an open heaven that no man could shut.

Whatever Moses had, they wanted. These were, what I can imagine to be thousands of women, sold out, determined to fight for God's Kingdom. This was an overflow of the gratitude they had for being set free from bondage. Just like these women, we should be grateful that we have been set free from sin and selfishness. Because they were so fixated on heaven, earthly things took a back seat and lost the prominence they once had. These worshipping warriors had their ear to the door and probably overheard that there was a need for materials to build the tabernacle. Out of their selflessness, they did what they could do to help by donating their hand-held mirrors made of bronze. It must have taken thousands of mirrors to have enough bronze to construct the laver and its pedestal as the scripture says.

Their sacrifice provided the materials needed for one of the sacred pieces of furniture to be placed inside the tabernacle that was soon to be built. Because these women were worshippers and intercessors their ears were opened to the needs of the tabernacle, and they met the need by donating the most valuable object some might think a woman could possess, her mirror.

MIRROR, MIRROR

To a woman, our mirror is the means by which we see our reflection. It can be our best friend or worst enemy. And sometimes, what we see there can determine the emotional status for the rest of our day. If we have wrinkles, crinkles, pimples and bags then we're miserable. We will want to stay in bed and hide or be compelled to keep putting concealer on to hide the blemishes.

The mirrors that these warring women donated were not made of reflective glass like we think of today. They were highly polished bronze by which they could see their reflection. The women in Egypt wore their mirrors around their neck as they visited their temple used for idolatrous practices.

In Exodus 12:36 it tells us that the children of Israel left with the riches of Egypt. That's probably how God's people got the mirrors in the first place. Yet they gave up something they loved for someone they loved even more than they loved themselves. These women traded the culture of Egypt for the culture of heaven. Removing the mirror that hung around their neck, weighing them down, and donating it so they could look up! That's what worship looks like. Much like Mary of Bethany, who poured out a pint of pure ointment that would be worth $48,000 in today's economy. That's $3,000 per ounce poured out on Jesus' feet as an act of worship. And our Heavenly Father gave up His one and only Son whom He loved for you and for me. Devotion and adoration equals sacrifice.

> Devotion and adoration equals sacrifice.

Most importantly these bronze mirrors were transformed into the laver, the first holy vessel you encountered in the Tabernacle. It stood between the entrance and the Presence. This sacred washbasin had fresh water poured into it everyday. The priests had to wash their hands and feet before they could approach God on behalf of the people, otherwise there would be death (Exodus 30:20). The laver speaks of our need of daily cleansing if communing with God is to be maintained. The laver, because it was constructed with highly polished bronze, allowed the priests to see their reflection, but it wasn't their outer reflection God was concerned about. God didn't need them to fix their hair or shave. It was for them to see their inner reflection.

INNER REFLECTION

The purpose of seeing their outer reflection when they entered the Tabernacle was so they would in turn reflect upon their shortcomings, downfalls, and the attitudes that needed to be reshaped. Thank God the laver had fresh water every day.

Applying the principal we know that the Old Testament is the New Testament concealed and the New Testament is the Old Testament revealed, we can look at what the bible tells us in Ephesians 5:26-27 about how Christ cleanses us by the washing of the Word. The Word is our sacred washbasin that provides fresh water daily to cleanse our spots. When we are not cleansed we encounter spiritual death. In James 1:23 the Word is also our sacred mirror. It shows us our identity, revealing who we are and whose we are. But it also is there to reveal our shortcomings and deals with our sin, showing us our true self. It allows us to go to God daily so He can fix us. Our mirror should not only be a place where we see our issues, but also where we realize that God is willing and able to correct and fix our blemishes.

As we mature and grow in our relationship with the Lord we should start to see a trade off where the importance or the condition of the outer man takes a back seat to the importance of the inner man. We willingly trade the prominence of the mirror that reflects the outer for the mirror that reflects the inner. So instead of being fixated on our reflection and taking selfies that say, "Look at me—Look at me!" We now hold up the mirror of God's Word taking inner selfies asking, "Holy Spirit, how am I doing? God, I need an adjustment, a little nip and tuck, a little plumping in that area." It's great to know what's trending but we must keep our finger on the pulse of heaven and know what's happening in heaven. Literally "what's up?"

In the Amplified Bible 1 Peter 3:3-4 (AMP) reads, *"Your adornment must not be merely external—with interweaving and elaborate knotting of the hair, and wearing gold jewelry, or [being superficially pre-occupied with] dressing in expensive clothes; but let it be [the inner beauty of] the hidden person of the heart, with the imperishable quality and unfading charm of a gentle and peaceful spirit, [one that is calm and self-controlled, not overanxious, but serene and spiritually mature] which is very precious in the sight of God."*

Before I go on let me say that years ago we thought that "holy" meant "homely," the homelier the holier, which turned out to be all about the outside. Although, I don't recommend going to the other extreme, forgetting the inner and concentrating more on the outer, the reality is that it should be a balance of outside and inside. Holy to me means "wholly devoted" inside and outside, through and through. The warring women in Exodus 38:8 traded their mirrors for worship warfare because God's bidding cannot be done with a mirror hung around our necks weighing us down.

> *"Charm and grace are deceptive, and [superficial] beauty is vain, but a woman who fears the*

Lord [reverently worshiping, obeying, serving, and trusting Him with awe-filled respect], she shall be praised." Proverbs 31:30 (AMP)

I believe we can turn the paradigm of the culture and show the world what real women of God look like! I believe all God wants is to see His reflection in our lives. We are God's mirror!

AGELESS QUESTIONS

1. Have you ever thought of yourself as a "sacred residence" where God dwells?

_____

_____

_____

_____

_____

_____

_____

2. Write in your own words the difference between the Tent of
   Meeting and the Tabernacle and how they play out in our
   every day life.

   _____

   _____

   _____

   _____

   _____

   _____

   _____

   _____

3. How important is your personal mirror to you and how
   does it affect your daily life?

   _____

   _____

   _____

_____

_____

_____

_____

_____

_____

4. How important is the "mirror" of God's Word to you and how does it affect your daily life?

_____

_____

_____

_____

_____

_____

_____

CHAPTER EIGHT

AGELESS = COMMUNITY

*"I yearn to come and be face-to-face with you and get to
know you. For I long to impart to you the spiritual gift
that will
empower you to stand strong in your faith. Now, this
means
that when we come together and are side-by-side, something wonderful will be released. We can expect to be
co-encouraged and co-comforted by each other's faith."*

Romans 1:11-12 (TPT)

YEARS AGO I left the tiny church I was attending nearby
to go to The Brooklyn Tabernacle, which with a few
hundred people seemed enormous to me compared to the
fifty people in my neighborhood church. Even though this
was way out of my comfort zone, we knew the Holy Spirit
was leading us. My husband worked on Sundays, so I had to
learn how to drive in order to be able to attend. At the time,
I had a two year old and a newborn. Making it to church
with two babies and a forty-five minute drive on the highway
wasn't easy. Then there was the task of finding a parking spot

not only on sunny days but also when there was rain, sleet, hail and snow. But the spitfire that I am, I was determined to push through whatever obstacle might cross my path, with my tiny bundles of joy, just to meet with the Lord.

A strong desire to get to know the people at the church began to stir within my soul, so I asked the Lord to show me how to accomplish what felt like a ginormous feat. What should I do? How would I go about it? Fear wanted to creep in. Would I be accepted? Would they like our family? After enough doubt and wondering, I decided it was time for action. I would pray every Sunday during the worship time, "Lord show me who I should invite to my house today" and He always did. I would approach whomever God had highlighted to me at the end of the service and say, "Hi, my name is Maria, would you like to come to my house for lunch and then we can come back to church for the evening service?" Almost always people accepted my invitation. I invited whosoever the Holy Spirit led me to. It didn't matter if they were married, single, young or not so young. They came in all sorts of shades and shapes. I would pack them into my station wagon and off we would go. Forty-five minutes back to my home and of course another forty-five minutes back to church for the evening service.

My husband worked in his father's food business at the time, and he would bring home raviolis, stuffed shells, marinara sauce, meatballs and cannoli. I would put a huge pot of water on the stove to cook the raviolis, and heat up the stuffed shells and meatballs in the oven. We would laugh and sometimes cry but God cemented us together with our in-home guests. Every week I would repeat the process over again. On Christmas Eve we would have over one hundred people squeezed into my living room, dining room and kitchen. We sang and had holy community.

No man is
an island to
himself;
we were
created to
do life with
one another.

No man is an island to himself; we were created to do life with one another. Genesis 2:18 states, *"It's not good for the man to be alone. I will make a helper who is just right for him."* Though this verse is speaking about the union between a man and a woman it also makes it clear that we were never intended to do life alone, and that we need help from one another. We have heard it said that there is strength in numbers yet I've noticed a trend in our modern society where community has become more and more impersonal and we've created a culture where we protect our personal space. As helpful as social media and modern technology can be, I feel it has caused us to become faceless, making it easy for us to avoid human contact or getting involved in matters that might cost us our time and energy.

To take it a step further, streaming church online has started to replace gathering together with other believers to worship and experience the presence of the Lord. While doing this on occasion might be necessary, making it a habit can be detrimental to your spiritual wellbeing. I understand, as a woman that raised three kids, that staying home and viewing a service in the comfort of your pajamas is more convenient. My concern is that once we replace *convenience* for *community* we begin forfeiting the benefits found in Acts 2:46.

The Merriam-Webster Dictionary defines *community* as groups of people with a common characteristic or interests living together within a larger society.[18] Some thoughts that stand out following the definition are:

- Common Character = Likeness

- Social Activity = Fellowship

- Synonyms = Body, bunch, circle, clan, clique, network, pack, gang

THE IMPORTANCE OF COMMUNITY

I don't know if you've noticed, but it seems to me that the cry of our time, other than "Where is my place," is "I need community." I don't think I've heard that word used in my entire lifetime more than in the last year. It is certainly a legitimate desire to want to be part of something bigger than yourself, yet also wanting to feel like you are a necessary part, a legitimate piece of a puzzle connected to likeminded people. Community is an imperative part of the church. After all scripture says that the apostles gave themselves to prayer, the word, communion and fellowship. Were these a coincidence? I think not, nothing in God's word is random. I like to call these the four spiritual food groups:

> Community is an imperative part of the church.

1. Prayer = vegetables.

2. The Word = meat

3. Communion = starch or grains

4. Fellowship = dessert

Many years ago the Holy Spirit showed me something very profound that convicted me. As I watched my young children interact around the dinner table I realized that while they were eating the meat, vegetables, and starch there wasn't much interaction. Yet when the dessert come out they started to open up about their day, connecting with us and with one another. I learned things about their friends, teachers and even themselves during the dessert time. It was then that I began to realize that I was strong in three of the categories, but I wasn't well balanced in all four. I was strong in prayer, the word and the importance of communion but I was lacking when it came to fellowship with other believers. Fellowship or community, as it is now referred to, is a necessary part of our Christian walk and shouldn't be undervalued. Our souls need quality time with other believers where we can commune and laugh together, because laughter is good medicine for the soul (Proverbs 17:22). It's within community that the walls of judgment come tumbling down, and we're able to see our own frailties through someone else's struggle, to see each other's needs and walk with one another rather than just throw a scripture at each other.

The apostle Paul recognized the importance of community. As a matter of fact he takes it a step farther and talks about a face-to-face encounter, a chance to look into the eyes of a like-minded community so that something "wonderful" can be released. He states, "I want to get to know you." In other words, where there is true community we get to know one another, therefore, we can expect to be co-encouraged and co-comforted as we are standing side-by-side. Paul realized he needed the body and the body needed him. He wasn't the end all, be all, he was just a part of the all. He wanted to know them and he wanted them to know him. This reality leaves me in awe.

I understand the great need to be connected to like-minded people but the question we are faced with is, "Who will start the process?" Remember the old song, "If You Can Use Anything Lord You Can Use Me?" We love to sing that song but the difficulty is putting feet to those words. Sometimes I think it's easier to go to the mission field than to invite someone over for a cup of coffee. We have tons of people sitting in church waiting to be invited instead of being the invitee.

The Holy Spirit is asking, "Who will go for me?" It says in Proverbs 18:24 (KJV, *paraphrased*), *"If you want to have friends, you must show yourself friendly."*

Going back to my early years at Brooklyn Tabernacle where I had made a habit of inviting people to my home every week. This went on for a few years and I would pray for the Lord to show me who I should invite that day. But this one particular day was different, I heard a voice say, "You have invited people to your house all these years, but you have never been invited." Those words went deep into my heart like a sword. I felt like I had been cut to the core. I agreed with that accusatory voice, and when the service was over I didn't invite anyone over. As a matter of fact, I stood there watching as the people were waving goodbye to me on their way out of the sanctuary. My children were pulling on my skirt and asking me "who are we taking home?" I kept telling them to shush. I walked to my car wounded and offended, tears streaming down my face. Putting the key in the car door I said to the Holy Spirit as I was sniffling loudly, "Lord, do you see I've been inviting all these years and no one has ever invited me?" The Holy Spirit answered me as clear as a bell, "I didn't bring you here to be invited, I brought you here to invite and you have now missed a week of doing my will. Don't let it happen again." Whoa!!! That was the rebuke of a lifetime. As a side note, you need to know how impossible it would have been for me to be invited to someone else's house. We only had one car and I had to go home in order to pick up my husband so we could get back for the evening service. Pity parties and the accusations of the enemy oftentimes make little sense except to get us to cease doing God's will.

Pity parties and the accusations of the enemy oftentimes make little sense except to get us to cease doing God's will.

How many of us have lost our focus? How many of us have lost our purpose obsessing over what hasn't been done for us, instead of focusing on all we have received by serving the Lord week after week, year after year? How many of us have listened to the lies of the enemy and have been sidetracked? How many are stuck in the fear of being rejected? You need to know this and don't ever forget it...some of us are called to be the initiators, givers, mentors, moms and dads. Somebody has got to start the process. We will probably get very little thanks for what we do, but not to worry, because our thanks will come from the one who will someday say, "Well done my good and faithful servant!" Your reward will also be to see the children that you have been given charge over grow up and become the initiators, givers, mentors and moms and dads. They have you as their example. You can't ask for more than that. In Malachi 4:6 (NIV) it is written, *"He will turn the hearts of the parents to their children, and the hearts of the children to their parents."* Notice it's the parent's heart that turns first, then the children's heart follows. Thus together both will be co-encouraged and co-comforted. Surely God knows what He is doing!

AGELESS QUESTIONS

1. Do you have a strong Christian community? Describe how that community affects your personal life and spiritual growth.

_____

_____

_____

_____

_____

_____

_____

_____

_____

_____

_____

2. The believers in the New Testament knew the importance of hospitality. Read the following four scriptures in the NIV and write out the theme that they all communicate: 1 Peter 4:9; Hebrews 13:2; Romans 12:13; 3 John 1:8.

_____

_____

_____

_____

_____

_____

_____

_____

_____

_____

_____

_____

3. Would you consider yourself to be hospitable? Give an example of how you show hospitality to others.

_____

_____

_____

_____

_____

_____

_____

_____

_____

_____

_____

_____

_____

4. Read 1 Corinthians 6:11-13. What might prevent a person from "opening wide their heart" to other believers?

_____

_____

_____

_____

_____

_____

_____

_____

_____

_____

_____

_____

_____

_____

AGELESS

5. Jesus' community was very diverse. Do you embrace different types of people into your community or do you tend to stick to "your own kind?" Explain.

_____

_____

_____

_____

_____

_____

_____

_____

_____

_____

_____

_____

142

6. Have you replaced *convenience* for *community*? If so, how has it impacted your spiritual and emotional growth?

_____

_____

_____

_____

_____

_____

_____

_____

_____

_____

_____

_____

_____

_____

CHAPTER NINE

AGELESS = FRUITFUL

"Joseph named his second son Ephraim, for he said,
'God has made me fruitful in the land of my grief."

Genesis 41:52

RECENTLY I TORE my meniscus and had to have knee surgery. A few moments before the surgery my doctor came in and told my husband and me that he had the same surgery last year and the day after he was up and out of bed. He went on to say that he drove himself to Home Depot to pick up a few things. That was very surprising to me, the fact that he was up and out in 24 hours. Since I was having surgery on my right knee, the leg that is involved in driving, it was an encouragement to think that I would be able to get around the very next day.

Once the surgery was over, true to form, I cannot even wake up. Hours passed and when I finally did wake up I was dizzy and nauseous. After some time my husband carefully helps me into the car to take me home. Not only had my knee been injected with pain medicine, I was still coming off the effects of the anesthesia which made me sleep until the next day. When I awoke I was in excruciating pain, my knee was swollen like a balloon and I assure you driving to Home Depot or anywhere else for that matter was the last thing on my mind. I was unable to put any pressure on my leg, much less stand without letting out a loud cry. I thank God for my husband who waited on me hand and foot. A week later, I was scheduled to go have the stitches removed from my incision. The nurse practitioner took one look and confirmed that it wasn't my imagination; my knee was swollen and filled with fluid. "You must still be in pain," she said. The doctor then arrives in the exam room and quickly asks how I'm feeling? I told him, "I'm in pain and I cannot bend my knee, and I cannot imagine making a trip to Home Depot." He turned and smiled at me. Then he said, "I did go to the store the next day, but I was in a lot of pain, which lasted a number of weeks, as I suspect your pain will last." I thought to myself, then why did you tell me that I would be up and out in a day? If I'm honest, I was a bit upset with him. I know he thought he was encouraging me but his words did just the opposite, they discouraged me. Every day post surgery when I woke up and still couldn't move my knee I thought there must be something wrong with me, and I wondered why I was being such a baby? I kept trying to put pressure on my knee, thinking that would help, but it made it worse. Now that I knew there was a process to my healing, I could bear the pain.

THE PROCESS TO HEALING

This same principle can also be applied to our spiritual walk. For those of us who have experienced some difficult stuff, we must be careful not to make it seem to those who are younger in the Lord that they will be going to "Home Depot" the next day. We have to make sure they understand that accepting the Lord today does not guarantee that they will have a perfect tomorrow or a stellar life. Explaining that there is a *real process* to healing and it's going to take some time before they are able to forgive their enemies, or change their habits, and the thoughts they think is a service we can provide. Saints are not made overnight; it takes a lifetime. The Holy Spirit enrolls us in His school of sanctification and being the godly counselor that He is, full of wisdom, patience and grace, will make sure we all graduate. But I assure you, not one of us can skip any of the course work. He's the true teacher but He does have "teacher aids" and we are the Helper's helpers!

> Saints are not made overnight; it takes a lifetime.

Genesis 45:1-4 states: "Joseph could stand it no longer. There were many people in the room, and he said to his attendants, 'Out, all of you!' So he was alone with his brothers when he told them who he was. Then he broke down and wept. He wept so loudly the Egyptians could hear him, and word of it quickly carried to Pharaoh's palace.

'I am Joseph!' he said to his brothers. 'Is my father still alive?' But his brothers were speechless!

> *They were stunned to realize that Joseph was standing there in front of them. 'Please, come closer,' he said to them. So they came closer. And he said again, 'I am Joseph, your brother, whom you sold into slavery in Egypt.'"*

When you read this, do you think this is the seventeen-year-old Joseph who first had a dream, or a mature Joseph that had been placed in the refiner's fire and had come forth as gold?

Imagine this: A wife hires a hit man to kill her husband. She then meets the hit man in a parking lot (usually a Wal-Mart for some strange reason) to pay him the rest of the money because she believes the dastardly deed has already been done. As she is handing over the money she sees her husband across the way. How do you think her husband would react? Do you think he would say, "Arrest her and throw away the key?"

When he sees his brothers, the ones that had sold him into slavery, Joseph says, *"But don't be upset, and don't be angry with yourselves for selling me to this place. It was God who sent me here ahead of you to preserve your lives. This famine that has ravaged the land for two years will last five more years, and there will be neither plowing nor harvesting. God has sent me ahead of you to keep you and your families alive and to preserve many survivors."*

Words cannot describe this scene, the pain, agony and guilt. Joseph holds all the cards and could have played them anyway he chose, but instead Joseph chose mercy. Not only does he allow them to live, he refuses to allow them to bear any of the blame and guilt. He encourages them not to grieve or be angry with themselves. Isn't that remarkable? We might forgive, but we want those who have wronged us to, at the very least, feel bad. How does years of mistreatment result in extreme kindness, mercy and amazing grace. John 12:24 says, *" I tell you the truth, unless a kernel of wheat is planted in the soil and dies, it remains alone. But its death will produce many new kernels—a plentiful harvest of new lives."* Unless the seed of self falls and bows prostrate there can be no life.

Using the illustration of the process of seed being bowed down I would like us to see how Joseph's life mirrors the process.

SEED FACTS

Seed Fact #1: *All seed must die ... no death, no fruit!* Inside of the seed is the fruit that is masked by a hard outer shell. That shell is called the protective seed coat. It serves as a wall of protection. It protects the core, the embryo. Just like our outer shell protects our spirit. The protective coat is only valuable in the beginning until the farmer decides it is fruit bearing time. Now because the fruit can't produce life in the spotlight or in its "protective package" it has to be placed in the dirt. Buried in utter darkness. Manure is placed on top of it. Think about it, manure is someone else's waste. The only way for the seed to shed its outer coat is when someone else's stinky stench is piled on top of it. Some days the sun beats down, other days the rain drenches it while the darkness rots it. Through this necessary process the hard outer coat disintegrates and comes apart at the seams. The outer shell has sacrificed itself so the life on the inside can sprout and take root. If you were to dig back in the ground you wouldn't find a trace of the outer shell. Do you see the symbolism of our spiritual life in the process of the seed? Trials come and other people's stinky stuff gets dumped on us while the heat of discouragement beats us down. Sometimes it rains so torrential you don't even know how you will survive. It's dark, lonely and scary but somehow we understand that opposition brings change. We yield knowing something greater is being birthed. In losing ourselves, we find Him (Jesus).

Joseph's journey started with a dream that turned into a nightmare for a season. That dream could have never come to fruition until he was first placed in the dirt, in the pit. That pit was his coffin. It was the burial service and his farewell party. Although his physical coat was stripped from him unwillingly, he willingly had to shed the coat of self for a greater purpose. He was buried underneath his brothers' manure, but in that dark place that manure turned into fertilizer. Joseph goes on to bear fruit that would feed two nations.

Seed Fact #2: *Not all seed dies and bears fruit.*

Although they are planted in the same soil, same environment, the protective shell of some seeds will not yield, break or crack. Those seeds never turn into anything. If you dig it up you will find the seed covered with slugs and maggots.

I was ministering at a conference and the worship on the first night was glorious. We were all singing our hearts out and surrendering ourselves to the Lord in a fresh way. The next morning there was a breakfast and my assistant, Penny, was in line to put her bread into the four-slice toaster. Behind her in line was the worship leader from the night before. Penny puts her two slices in the slots, and just as the woman behind her goes to put her two slices into the toaster another woman jumps in front and places her two slices into the toaster and walks away. The woman who was cut from the toaster line was outraged. She took that aggressive woman's toast out of the toaster and proceeded to put her toast in. "Ha! Who does she

The gift is
exactly that,
a gift from
God dropped in
your lap, but
the fruit of
the spirit must
be developed,
over time
through a
process

think she is?" This worship leader was now singing a different tune.

Penny quickly takes her own toast out and puts in the bread of the woman who cut the line. The other woman looked at Penny as though she were an alien and said, "Why would you do that?" Penny answered, "It's the godly thing to do!" As far as I could see, they hadn't said goodbye to themselves. They were still dressed in their outer shell, and hadn't given themselves a funeral service yet. They would proudly say, "I don't smoke, party or go out dancing but let me assure you that I don't let anybody put their toast in the toaster ahead of me!"

It is a disservice in our church community when we place more value on the gifts of the spirit than on the fruit of the spirit. The gift is exactly that, a gift from God dropped in your lap, but the fruit of the spirit must be developed, over time through a process. There is not one of us that can bypass this painful process of dying to self. Joseph believed what he lived and lived what he believed.

Seed Fact #3: Farmers say the most difficult part of the process is what they call the "break-through" process.

At this stage the plant is fully developed on the inside. All the work that was done in secret is ready for public debut to bless others. But it's met with great opposition as it faces the greatest barrier. The same dirt that was part of the process for growth and advancement now becomes part of the process to hold it down. The hard ground above tries to keep the plant stuck below. The plant must fight to become what it was created to be if it wants to survive. It must fight through for the breakthrough. It must dig its heels in the ground and push its head into the light, just like a mother in labor being encouraged to push and push.

Oftentimes this is where we lose the battle. The resistance is too much so we settle to live in the dirt. The enemy doesn't want us to put our fruit on display so that others can taste and see that the Lord is good. He's fine with the funeral service, but he certainly doesn't want a resurrection service. These obstacles are opportunities where those of us who are older in the Lord come in, because we know what it's like to be thrown in a pit of despair, we've been betrayed, or lied about or even abandoned. But because someone talked us out of the pit, we can stand our ground and encourage those younger in the Lord to keep on pushing forward. We can't allow them to make that pit their home.

I'm sure Joseph had flashbacks. I'm sure the sight of his brothers wanted to send him spiraling back down into that pit of un-forgiveness. He had to fight through for the breakthrough that only came when he rose above the dirt of the past and blessed his brothers. It seems that Joseph was forgotten from the moment he was placed in that pit. He was alone in a foreign land, falsely accused and forsaken in a prison but thank God we don't have to fight alone.

We are not in a foreign land. We are amongst our brothers and sisters. God has seen fit to place us in the body of Christ, the family of God. We don't have to be afraid of betrayal or being lied about, because God's word says that He has not given us a spirit of fear. Those of us that have shed pounds of flesh, self and pain, can share our struggles and triumphs with one another and be there for one another in the body of Christ.

Seed Fact #4: *What goes into the ground looks nothing like what comes out of the ground.*

An apple seed doesn't look anything like a big, juicy, shiny, luscious, tasty apple. When Joseph was reunited with his brothers he looked nothing like what he looked like when they abandoned him. If you read the full story in Genesis, you'll notice that when Joseph had his first and second dream he was full of himself. He was bragging to his brothers and his father about how they would all bow down to him. His father loved him the most and gave him a special coat that made Joseph proud and most likely a bit obnoxious. It also made his brothers resentful and angry. Now stripped of his man-made coat; he was clothed in humility. He definitely didn't want anyone to bow before him. His heart was now bowed before the Lord.

This process is necessary for every single one of us. We shouldn't forget who we used to be and the way we used to act. Let's remember all the mercy and grace God has had upon us. Keeping this in mind, we will be patient, speaking the truth with love to one another always having their good in mind. In the Body of Christ, we need a true revelation that we are a family and must look out for one another, as well as being willing to learn from one another. As Christians there are family values that need to be passed on from generation to generation and need to be accepted regardless of the present day culture.

As important as family is in our lives, it can also get a little messy. We can tend to step on one another's toes at times but that's because we really care. There's nothing easy about the different roles and personalities within the family structure. Whether it's parent to child or sibling-to-sibling, there are so many dynamics that go into how we relate to one another.

At times we might really hurt one another with our words or actions but like the song by Sister Sledge says, "We Are Family" (I know I'm dating myself) and we should never give up on one another.

Those of us with more life (and spiritual life) experience and development need to be patient with the ones that are younger. I admit that's not always easy to do. When you're young you never think of yourself as lacking experience and development. Taking advice does not come easy because you think you know what's best for you. It

> It takes a certain measure of wisdom to properly give advice but it also takes wisdom to accept advice.

takes a certain measure of wisdom to properly give advice but it also takes wisdom to accept advice. Proverbs 13:10 states, *"Pride leads to conflict; those who take advice are wise."* I would have given anything to have an older sister that looked out for me and protected me from the dangers that await us girls out in the real world.

EXPERIENCE & DEVELOPMENT

One of the challenges of being young is that the culture we live in does not value being young and applies pressure on young people to grow up too soon. I see this happening in the church as well, with young believers expected to mature overnight. False maturity leads to an appearance of being mature without the spiritual experience and development (infrastructure) required to live mature. That type of pressure only leads to failure.

Wisdom is
proven by
our actions.
Charisma gets
us in the room
but character
keeps us there.

The Bible says in 1 Timothy 5:22 don't lay hands on anyone suddenly. A person needs time to grow and a time to be proven. Wisdom is proven by our actions. Charisma gets us in the room but character keeps us there. The church has often-times participated in making people feel and appear more developed than they are. We have sensationalized the gifts and have minimized the fruit. Gifts have nothing to do with fruit. Just because someone is an excellent communicator or worship leader certainly doesn't mean they have integrity or that they are the best person to trust.

The development of character is partly the work of the Holy Spirit and partly ours as His helper. The younger under-developed seed must not resist thinking they can bypass this important process. If Joseph couldn't bypass the process then neither can we. He had the favor of his father and he also had the gift of interpreting dreams yet he lacked humility. Joseph bragged about the dreams to his brothers and his father while wearing the special coat of many colors, thinking that his favor with God and man would allow him the luxury to rush ahead of the process. He thought the dream would come to pass the next day but if you know the story then you know that before there could be any bowing before him, God had to break him and bend him, mold him and shape him. Years later when his brothers finally bowed before him Joseph wept in humility because his heart was now void of himself, bowed before the Lord. Choice fruit had been developed in him.

May we allow the process of character to transpire in all our lives! May we who are older in the Lord have the incredible fruit of patience that overflows and touches the lives around us allowing the divine process of sanctification to have its way!

AGELESS QUESTIONS

1. If you are a seasoned believer, have you ever put unrealistic spiritual expectations on someone who was younger either in age or in their faith? How did those expectations cause that person to respond to you?

_____

_____

_____

_____

_____

_____

_____

_____

_____

_____

_____

_____

_____

2. If you are younger either in age or faith, do you welcome advice from someone who is more experienced and developed? How has that choice affected your life?

_____

_____

_____

_____

_____

_____

_____

_____

_____

_____

_____

_____

_____

_____

3. Have you ever felt betrayed or rejected by a family member or close friend? How did their actions affect your relationship?

_____

_____

_____

_____

_____

_____

_____

_____

_____

_____

_____

_____

4. In your personal faith journey, do you focus more on your
   gifting or your character [fruit]? What do you think others
   notice first about your life—your gifts or your fruit?

_____

_____

_____

_____

_____

_____

_____

_____

_____

_____

_____

_____

_____

5. Which Seed Fact was the most eye opening to you and why?

_____

_____

_____

_____

_____

_____

_____

_____

_____

_____

_____

_____

_____

_____

6. So many believers love the story of Joseph. In your own words describe what you think is the most powerful part of his story.

_____

_____

_____

_____

_____

_____

_____

_____

_____

_____

_____

_____

_____

NOTES

1. Psalm 34:8

2. *Miriam-Webster*, s.v. "Surrender" accessed June 20, 2019, https://www.merriam-webster.com/dictionary/surrender.

3. *Bible Study Tools*, s.v. "Neos'," accessed June 20, 2019, https://www.biblestudytools.com/lexicons/greek/kjv/neos.html.

4. *Bible Study Tools*, s.v. "Kainos," accessed June 20, 2019, https://www.biblestudytools.com/lexicons/greek/nas/kainos.html.

5. *Miriam-Webster*, s.v. "Weary," accessed June 20, 2019, https://www.merriam-webster.com/dictionary/weary.

6. Micah 7:19

7. Luke 17:12-19

8. Luke 22:34

9. Matthew 26:47-50

10. *BrainyQuote®*, s.v. "John Knox," accessed June 21, 2019, https://www.brainyquote.com/quotes/john_knox_378457.

11. *FaithGateway.com*, s.v. "Chris Hodges," accessed June 21, 2019, https://www.faithgateway.com/the-daniel-dilemma-in-the-world-but-not-of-it/.

12. *Wikiquote*, s.v. "Francis of Assisi," accessed June 21, 2019, htps://en.wikiquote.org/wiki/Francis_of_Assisi.

13. *Miriam-Webster*, s.v. "Gratitude" accessed June 21, 2019, https://www.merriam-webster.com/dictionary/gratitude.

14. *BrainyQuote®*, s.v. "Marcus Tullius Cicero," accessed June 21, 2019, https://www.brainyquote.com/quotes/marcus_tullius_cicero_122152.

15. *Greater Good Mgazine*, s.v. "Gratitude," accessed June 21, 2019, https://greatergood.berkeley.edu/article/item/what_stops_gratitude.

16. Ibid.

17. *Bible Study Tools*, s.v. "Tsaba'," accessed July 2, 2019, https://www.biblestudytools.com/lexicons/hebrew/kjv/tsaba.html.

18. *Miriam-Webster*, s.v. "Community" accessed July 2, 2019, https://www.merriam-webster.com/dictionary/community.

ACKNOWLEDGMENTS

I would like to first and foremost thank the Father who has loved me, Jesus who died for me and the Holy Spirit who breathes life in me every day of my life.

I want to thank my precious husband, Michael, for giving me the time to pursue Gods call on my life and for continuously writing me love notes with words of affection and encouragement.

I want to thank my amazing children and my awesome grandchildren for always making me feel *Ageless*.

I would like to thank my incredible friend, Michele Amodio, for tirelessly reading these chapters, making much needed corrections and doing whatever needed to be done to get this manuscript into book form without ever complaining.

I would like to thank Jana Burson who used the amazing gift God has given her to edit this book.

I would like to thank Renee Fisher and Nelly Murariu who masterfully know how to format plain pages and make it into a creative work of art.

ABOUT THE AUTHOR

 **MARIA DURSO** has served along-side her husband Michael in full time ministry since 1985. She is an intercessor, teacher and powerful speaker sharing the Good News of the Gospel all over the world.

Maria was born in 1950 and does not consider herself a *spring chicken,* or a chicken by any other name. She firmly believes that in order to serve the Lord you cannot have a yellow streak. You have to be *fearless.* You have to have a strong constitution to withstand the wiles of the enemy and the wild antics and attitudes of the various people you come in contact with. For the most part ministry is amazing. You get to be on the front lines and see people walk into the sanctuary one way and walk out changed. You get to be a part of their lives, teaching them and praying them through the many difficult challenges that life throws their way. You also gather an army of like-minded people who will stand with you through your night seasons.

Maria believes that the number one issue in the church at this time is seeing talented, gifted women feel out of place. She states, "The number one question that she hears as she travels to minister is 'where is my place?' She understands that there are seasons in life and this is definitely a season where younger creative, gifted and godly people are stepping up to the plate to fulfill their divine purpose. But that doesn't mean that the season of the mature woman is over, they are needed more now than ever.

Maria lives by the mantra that as long as we love people we will never be out of a job in the kingdom.

Maria wrote this book out of her strong conviction that every Christian has a divine duty to pour into someone else, a life that is emptier than your own. Mary had Elizabeth, Ruth had Naomi, Timothy had Paul, Joshua had Moses, and Esther had Mordecai. Otherwise we will dry up. Just like the Red Sea, everything flows in which makes it rich in minerals and nutrients, but there are no tributaries, input but no output.

No flowing out into a sea that is way vaster than itself.

This is the key to being ageless!

CPSIA information can be obtained
at www.ICGtesting.com
Printed in the USA
LVHW082324261121
704455LV00011B/1503

9 781692 523236